INFLUENTIAL SUSTAINABILITY PRACTICES

Insights for Holistic Development of Corporate World

DR. TRIPTI SHARMA,
DR. AVNI PATEL

INDIA • SINGAPORE • MALAYSIA

ISBN 979-8-89322-913-4

DEDICATION

I, dedicate this book to my parents Late Dr. Manjulata Sharma and Dr. Gopichand Sharma (National Award Winner). You both are an inspiration for me to hold faith in God while going through the uncertainties of life. This achievement is a tribute to your seamless efforts over many years where you chose to give me the best education. Your immense support, love, and encouragement incredibly played a pivotal role in keeping the "Never Say Die" spirit.

I also, dedicate this thesis to my husband Vidipt Chaturvedi who made sure that I completed the task of my doctoral journey within the set deadlines. His help and support eminently added a feather to my life.

Life is worthy when you have supporters who want you to rise and achieve great heights. I dedicate my thesis to all my well-wishers, yes, our dream came true we made it.

Abstract

Influential Sustainability Practices: Insights for Holistic Development of Corporate World is a book which is focusing on the Green Supply Chain Management Practices Adopted by the Manufacturing Companies of Gujarat"

Submitted By: Dr. Tripti Sharma, Assistant Professor, Ahmedabad Institute of Technology, Ahmedabad.

Supervised By: Dr. Avni Patel, PhD-Management, Assistant Professor-GLS University, Ahmedabad.

Keywords: GSCM, Green Practices, Manufacturing Companies, Drivers, Organizational Performance, Outcomes.

Background: In the era of globalization, Indian industries are facing pressure to green their supply chain at international and domestic levels. It is because of the reason that environmental concerns have gained more attention recently among Indian organizations, and still, it needs to recognize an adequately significant number of factors related to environmental and sustainable issues from industrial viewpoints. Green Supply Chain Management is an emerging aspect abiding which has brought a drastic change worldwide.

Sustainability Management is a blend of supply chain management practices and environmental considerations. It is playing a major role in sustaining the environment thereby enhancing the economic and ecological footprint of industries. Indian Industries are under tremendous compulsion from customers' environmental awareness and stricter environmental regulations to incorporate ethical and environmental considerations in all facets of traditional supply chain management. (Luthra et al., 2011; Mathiyazhagan et al., 2013, Mangla et al., 2014b). By adopting the GSCM Indian manufacturing companies can lead to resolvent of societal issues and scarcity of natural resources.

Aim: Theories of GSCM adoption and its implementation are majorly taking place in developed countries. However, studies related to GSCM are less often in India. Furthermore, a limited study has been carried out in Gujarat for the implementation of GSCM. The lack of prior research in manufacturing companies in Gujarat has motivated the researcher to undertake a detailed investigation of prevailing GSCM practices in Manufacturing Companies in Gujarat and to identify the impact of these practices on organizational performance.

Research Methodology: The research design of this study is Descriptive Research. At present, Descriptive Research involved the pre-planned and structured design by way of quantitative analysis through hypothesis testing and using a survey method through one-to - one approach. In the current research, a survey has been conducted through a primary study of 424 manufacturing companies. Data analysis covering SPSS and AMOS are employed for the analysis to check the awareness and investigate the impact of practices on the overall organizational performance.

Results & Discussion: As resultant the impact of green practices was established on the overall performance of the manufacturing companies of Gujarat state. The awareness of GSCM and the major practices followed by the companies are identified.

Conclusion: Exhaustive and comprehensive research across the manufacturing companies of Gujarat indicated a positive effect of the adoption of GSCM on the all-inclusive performance of the companies. This study concludes by establishing that GSCM practices directly and positively have an impact on organizational performance.

Scope for Further Study: The study has significant scope to the board base if it is carried out on manufacturing companies following GSCM in other states of India.

Table of Contents

Abbreviation

GSCM	Green Supply Chain Management
CSM	Corporate Social Responsibility
3Rs	Reduce, Reuse, Recycle
4Ps	Product, Price, Promotion, Place
5Rs	Reduce, Reuse, Recycle, Recover, Redesign
LCA	Life Cycle Assessment
LCC	Life Cycle Costing
EPR	Extended Producer Responsibility
SCM	Supply Chain Management
GRI	Global Reporting Initiative
WBCSD	World Business Council for Sustainable Development

Acknowledgment

"Gratitude is the sweetest thing in a seeker's life – in all human life. If there is gratitude in your heart, then there will be tremendous sweetness in your eyes." **Sri Chinmoy**

"Shree Ganeshaye Namah" Gratitude is a warm feeling of thankfulness towards the special individuals who supports you in flourishing and achieving your future endeavors. In my Ph.D. exploration, substantially many people played an eminent role in making me climb the ladder of submitting the thesis. It is my privilege to extend heartfelt gratification to them.

It gives me immense happiness and satisfaction to submit my Doctorate thesis titled, "A Study on Green Supply Chain Management Practices Adopted by the Selected Companies of Gujarat".

During my doctoral work, I have been receiving encouragement, support, and help from innumerable personalities. At this juncture, I would like to acknowledge with appreciation the contribution of all these people who have, in some way or other, helped and encouraged me during my doctorate study. I would like to take an opportunity to thank all of them without whom; a work of this nature would not have been possible.

First of all, I would like to acknowledge my deepest gratitude and a big thank you to my doctoral guide Professor Dr. Avni Patel, Assistant Professor, GLS University for her untiring support, help, and valuable guidance, which helped me in the successful completion of this study. At this moment I humbly pay my respect to her for developing me as a scholar.

At this moment I wish to convey my big thank you to Dr. Avni Desai, Dean, School of Doctoral Research and Innovation, GLS University for her unending support throughout my study.

I would also like to mention Dr. Dharmesh Shah, Registrar, of GLS University for his cordial support in the smooth conduct of the administration of my entire study process.

Also, I am so grateful to Dr. Pradeep Siwach (Pro Vice Chancellor of Chitkara University) who holds the belief in me and directed me to pursue a PhD.

A special thanks to experts and my RDC members Dr. Gurmeet Singh (Faculty- Associate Professor, GLS University) and Dr. Narayan Baser (Associate Professor at School of Petroleum Management, PDPU University) for continuous guidance, and expert support

during my research work. I cannot forget the endless support of both experts and panel members who guided me every time by giving their valuable suggestions when needed.

I would also like to thank Dr. Hemraj Verma (Dean Academics, DIT University), Dr. Atul Siva (Chandigarh University), Dr.Arun Aggarwal (Chitkara University), Prof. Suraj Shah (Chairperson -SAS-GUNI Global Centre for Analytics, Ganpat University) for expert advice.

My special thanks to Dr Hitesh Parmar who is the Guide of My Guide and spared his valuable time for reviewing my questionnaire and for imparting knowledge of SEM. Also, I extend heartfelt gratitude to Dr. Dhaval Mehta for providing beneficial knowledge of SEM.

Furthermore, a humble thanks to Dr. Hema Trivedi, Ph.D. program coordinator (Management) for her unconditional help and appropriate guidance during the entire research work.

Next, an exceptional big thanks to all Managing Heads of Manufacturing companies who were respondents to my study and spared their valuable time. The detailed investigation of my research was only possible through their support and response.

A very BIG THANKS to my father Dr Goipchand Sharma and my late mother Dr Manjulata Sharma who aspired me to carry never say die spirit and to face challenges with positive temperament and great zeal. Their preachings and guidance made my dream come true.

I express my gratitude to my husband Vidipt Chaturvedi for motivating me and managing the entire family during this journey. He stood as a pillar by providing his assistance and helping me in completing my target.

Lastly, I thank all connected people who directly and indirectly helped me to achieve my Ph.D. degree. They proved to be a blessing for those who supported the attainment of this goal and made my journey full of fruit-bearing experiences. I feel precious to be part of this experience.

Thank You, Happy Reading! ***– Tripti Sharma***

CHAPTER-1

Introduction

About 70% of the top businesses in their industries have prioritized sustainability in their work agendas during the last few years. Leading businesses' reports confirm that cooperation with supply chain (SC) actors is essential for the success of their sustainable activities. Green or sustainable supply chain management (SSCM) entails incorporating economic and environmental goals into the management of the supply chain's operational strategy. Such integration boosts financial return and profitability while reducing the carbon footprint (Herrmann, F. F., Barbosa-Povoa, A. P., Butturi, M. A., Marinelli, S., & Sellitto, M. A., 2021).

The effective implementation of eco-efficiency, renewable energy sources, and sustainable actions in the Supply chain, in innovation clusters, as well as in symbiotic industrial networks has been facilitated by green supply chain management (GSCM) in this context (Sellitto, M.A.; Camfield, C.G.; Buzuku, S., 2020). The majority of the prior study on GSCM has concentrated on how the implementation of operation administration and supply chain affects the environment and social sustainability. The GSCM structure and performance assessment are the two types of GSCM research subjects that have been indicated by prior studies (Ninlawan et al., 2010).

Prior studies showed that the context in which Green supply chain Management (GSCM) has operated and the forces behind GSCM adoption were diverse in recent years. Numerous types of literature have addressed the driving force behind GSCM practices in terms of sustainability practices, green manufacturing (Chuang & Yang, 2014; Ghazilla et al., 2015); green distribution (Strömberg et al., 2015); and reverse logistics (Akdoan & Coşkun, 2012) in the context of the GSCM conceptual framework. Munim et al. (2018) carried out an extensive evaluation of the GSCM literature using a bibliometric method. Their study made use of bibliometric analysis, which emphasizes the most-cited works and their influence. In the meantime, there is still a lack of systematic and comprehensive analysis that concentrates on the GSCM subject and chronology to summarise the present article on GSCM driving causes and important concerns and offer future research directions (Munim et al., 2018).

Numerous empirical studies have looked into what motivates a firm to extend green management standards and practices throughout its supply chain. GSCM can be influenced by community organizations, market demand, and the necessity to ensure complete compliance with stricter environmental standards (Darnall et al., 2008a; Nawrocka, 2008; Delmas and Toffel, 2004; Zhu and Sarkis, 2007).

The literature views the green supply chain (GSC) as an organizational component supporting the circular economy. In recent years, the pressure of legislation and consumer awareness has drawn the attention of many researchers and practitioners to the GSC. According to various academicians, integrating the environment into the supply chain can give businesses a competitive edge. All industries should take into account improving their environmental performance (EP), which is a significant source of pollution across its supply chain (Benzidia, S., Makaoui, N., & Bentahar, O., 2021). GSCM also includes considerations for supplier development to meet green purchasing requirements, warehousing, transportation, and stimulus for the adoption of environmental certifications like ISO 14000. Concerns about product design, use, reuse, disassembly, and final disposal are also included (Herrmann, F. F., Barbosa-Povoa, A. P., Butturi, M. A., Marinelli, S., & Sellitto, M. A., 2021). GSCM may help a firm perform better in terms of the environment and aid its competitive strategy as a result of its enhanced environmental reputation. Our research evaluates two strategies that a company might use to affect the environmental performance of its suppliers and, indirectly, of its manufacturing process or products: evaluating their environmental performance and asking that way of implementation of environmental measures. Internal strategic motivations can encourage an organization to adopt environmental practices concerning its supply chain in order to gain a competitive advantage because an analysis that concentrates on such external forces does not allow for a complete understanding of corporate ethics (Sharfman et al., 2009).

1.1 Concept of Supply Chain

A supply chain is the network of all the people, businesses, resources, tasks, and technological advancements involved in the production and distribution of a good. An entire supply chain, from the distribution of raw materials from the supplier to the producer to the final delivery to the customer, is included. The distribution channel refers to the portion of the supply chain that transports the final good from the manufacturer to the consumer.

Value chains and supply chains can be compared because they make different contributions to the final product. A supply chain's goal is to satisfy consumer demand. Worth chains aim to enhance a product's value beyond that which it already possesses. The value chain serves to offer the business a competitive edge in the market. In order to satisfy two somewhat different conceptions of "demand," supply chain management and value chain management collaborate to see the same fundamental process from two slightly different angles.

The administration of materials, data, and money as they flow through a process from supplier to manufacturer to wholesaler to retailer to customer is known as supply chain management

(SCM). The product flow, the information flow, and the financial flow are the three primary flows of the supply chain. These take place during the three key phases of strategy, planning, and operation. These flows must be coordinated and integrated as part of SCM both within and between businesses.

1.2 History of Supply Chain

Although the newspaper "The Independent" is credited with coining the phrase "supply chain" in 1905, the idea of a network of suppliers, producers/manufacturers, and customers existed for a very long period before that. The term "supply chain management" didn't come into use until the 1980s, therefore the profession is still in its infancy when compared to closely related disciplines like manufacturing, procurement, and logistics. Rum was the first product produced using a "truly worldwide supply network." In this instance, the sugarcane, which was imported from India, was grown in the Caribbean by slaves who had been transported from Africa, and the supply chain concluded at US distilleries. The formation of logistics as a distinct subject was influenced by ancient empires from Peru to Rome, which introduced roadways, organized labour, transportation, and armies. Considering the land, people, food, and property, all of them required a significant amount of organization.

Due to the scarcity of larger transit alternatives and the high expense of shipping commodities across the globe, all components of a supply chain were kept primarily local from these early times up until the 18th century. The number of commodities that could be delivered along any link in the supply chain increased enormously as shipping capabilities improved.

The advent of mass production on assembly lines in the late 1920s created the groundwork for supply chain management. The concept of creating consistent items at a wide scale with greater efficiency was first effectively applied by Ford, and it permanently altered trade and supply networks.

Until the late 18th century, when ship pulleys were produced in England and weapons were produced in America, mass manufacturing and the idea of replaceable parts had not yet been paired with specialization, continuous workflow, and division of labor.

Containerization, or container transportation, increased the amount of space available for commodities while simultaneously speeding up freight transit and lowering the cost. The speed improvement resulted from more efficient transport terminals and warehousing procedures. A new era of international trade was ushered in by the development of this transport method, which included loading and unloading cargo.

Another industry game-changer was barcoding, which was patented more than 20 years before being employed for the first time in the 1970s. The US National Association of Food Chains' standard mandating an identification number and subsequent study demonstrating significant increases in profit via "point scale scanning" served as catalysts for its adoption. The barcode might be used for "monitoring of the supply chain both globally and internationally" once it was modified to become an accepted worldwide standard.

The invention of the personal computer in the 1980s sparked the development of additional new technology that had a significant impact on supply chain management, including spreadsheets, optimization models, and algorithms that could forecast logistics problems in a supply chain. These addressed issues with planning, resource management, and forecasting while also improving the ability to see, store, and communicate information about the entire supply chain.

The development of systems like Enterprise Resource Planning systems, or ERPs, which were an expansion of the Electronic Data Interchange (EDI) systems established decades earlier, came in close succession with faster and more powerful computers. ERPs gave companies the ability to use software to manage every aspect of their operations, including automating corporate processes, centralizing information, controlling money, and monitoring performance. Before ERPs, it was common for firms to experience problems such as being unable to access information from many departments, which hindered growth, reduced efficiency, and resulted in overlooked mistakes.

Big data and social media use over the past 15 years have exposed unethical supply chain practices that were previously unknown to the public. Analytics today play an even more crucial part in supply chain management due to the push from all around the world to have ethical, sustainable supply chains as well as the constant search for greater efficiency.

The creation and widespread use of analytics has added monitoring as a new layer to supply chain management. To satisfy the expectations of stakeholders, supply chain management has had to use technology as product life cycles have shortened and efficiency levels have risen. Real-time monitoring is also being promoted, especially in light of the mounting public pressure to maintain sustainability and social responsibility.

The scope of a supply chain's management has expanded to encompass dealing with big data and having access to real-time visibility since all portions of a supply chain might now be subject to public or legal scrutiny.

1.3 History of Green Supply Chain

Environmental awareness has indeed grown over the past few decades. Global warming, the use of harmful substances, and the depletion of non-renewable resources are all issues that are becoming more well-known.

In addition, the government has launched programs to raise public awareness of this issue. incorporating green business practices into their operations, such as employing environmentally friendly raw materials, lowering their reliance on oil, and using recycled paper for packaging. Many organizational departments, including the delivery system, have adopted green concepts.

We are all aware that the Green Supply Chain Management (GSCM) has emerged in recent years. This concept encompasses all phases of production from the product's design to recycling, for example. Government, education, and other service-related industries can also benefit from GSCM training in addition to manufacturing.

The first paper on green supply was written by Navinchandra, D. (1988), who suggested using green design to lessen the impact of product waste. The same green design was developed and its framework was enhanced by Ashley, S. (1993), Allenby, S., Richards, D. (1994), and Zhang et al. (1997). Green literature also gave rise to the idea of reverse logistics, which is crucial to Green Operations. Some of these articles discuss the recycling of bottles and the use of plastics. A standardized strategy for minimizing electronic waste without affecting the environment was developed by Pohlen, T. L., & Farris, M. T. (1992); Stock, J. (1998); Tibben A. and Lembke, R. S., who also discussed the usage of plastics and bottle recycling in case studies and articles (2002). In their study on the Chinese manufacturing sector, Zhu, Q., and Sarkis, J., (2004) found that GSCM procedures sought to have a favorable association with environmental and economic performance. When Hsu, C. W., and Hu, A. H. (2008) investigated the function of green supply chain management in the electronic industry, they discovered that there had been little research on the efficacy and dependability of green supply systems. Twenty alternatives were prioritized using a fuzzy analytic hierarchy procedure by the author in nine electronic firms, and it was discovered that firms would place a strong emphasis on supplier management performance to manage a green supply chain.

Zhou, F. (2009) concluded that this management approach takes the environmental impact and effective resource usage in the entire supply chain into account. Ninlawan et al. (2010) researched Thailand's electronic industry's adoption of green supply chain management. In his study, he used 11 firms as a case study and conducted interviews and questionnaires with them to get their in-depth opinions on the current state of green activities, such as green production, green distribution, and reverse logistics. The Thai electronic industry's green supply chain was assessed based on its performance, green supply chain management procedures, and the drivers behind it. According to Wu et al. (2010), to improve the performance of green management, businesses should concentrate on the impact of immediate costs and benefits on knowledge transfer.

1.4 Benefits of GSCM

When it comes to greening the supply chain, it would be reasonable to consider merely prohibiting toxic chemical applications or minimizing environmental issues or waste. However, it involves much more than just simple use and pollution reduction.

As a result, advantages extend beyond fewer wasteful or hazardous consumption choices. The GSCM's guiding principles can be used in all divisions of the organization. The consequences of GSCM are felt everywhere, in both tangible and intangible ways.

Nevertheless, other studies highlighted the advantages of implementing the GSCM, (Stevels, 2002). He described the advantages of the GSCM in terms of several categories, including material, immaterial, and emotional, and in terms of diverse roles of distribution, including the environment and society.

The GSCM supports lower resource consumption by humans, lower cost of ownership for clients, lower cost of production for suppliers, and lower environmental burden used for the environment when it comes to material.

In terms of the trivial, GSCM helps eliminate prejudice and cynicism for the environment, fewer rejections for suppliers, easier production for manufacturers, convenience, and amusement for customers, and the best consent for society.

According to Duber-Smith (2005), there are ten reasons why a business must accept going green. These reasons include resource sustainability, target marketing, the ethical imperative, marketable and distribution network pressures, product differentiation and strategic edge, return on investment, adjusting to regulation and mitigating risk, company image, employee morale, and decreased costs/ increased efficiency.

1.5 Determinants of GSCM

1.5.1 The Factors That Influence a Firm's Decision to Implement Green Supply Chain Management

According to the research, there are two main categories of factors that influence GSCM adoption: "external forces," which are mostly pressures from stakeholders, and "internal factors," or a particular business-led strategy process. These vary depending on the origin of the "stimulus" that fosters the growth of GSCM processes, as well as their spread throughout the supply chain and sharing with clients and suppliers. Regarding "external variables," Di Maggio and Powell (1983) contend that three institutional mechanisms—normative, coercive, and mimetic—may have an impact on managerial decisions to implement environmental management efforts. Organizations are forced to conform to normative constraints, such as consumer demands, to be seen as more legitimate (Zhu and Sarkis, 2007). Additionally, several external parties may exert coercive pressure on businesses, depending on their power. For instance, government entities may influence whether businesses embrace environmental practices by enacting strict environmental regulations (Delmas, 2002). "Regulatory" pressures result from regulations to publicly publish information about an organization's environmental impact or from threats of fines and penalties for non-compliance (Konar and Cohen, 1997). Industrial associations and social and environmental care groups are additional examples (Henriques and Sadorsky, 1996). (Guler et al., 2002).These kinds of pressures can motivate managers to execute supply chain-focused strategic measures to improve their influence over supply chain decision processes, boost their external reputation, and enhance their marketability. Zhu and Sarkis (2007) recently evaluated the moderating role of institutional forces on the adoption of GSCM; their findings showed that enterprises under more regulatory pressure adopt green supply chain strategies. Limiting the examination to just "institutional pressures" prevents us from fully comprehending why businesses operating in the same market or sector choose various strategies despite being subject to the same organizational pressures (Delmas and Toffel, 2004). Managers may choose measures that try to develop, rationalize, implement, and better manage business relationships in the distribution network for strategic reasons that are independent of external impulses. The following are some examples of these factors:

1. The involvement of inter-firm cooperation to find and implement continual improvement, both on the input side of the product life cycle (e.g., procurement, cooperation with primary suppliers) and on the output side (e.g., organizing recycling, information on proper use for final consumers, etc.). These are put into practice to cut costs and boost productivity (Corbett and DeCroix, 2001);
2. It is possible to choose service providers who have implemented good environmental practices (i.e., by implementing an environmental management system that conforms with ISO 14001 regulations) to lessen the environmental hazards connected to their operations (Sarkis, 2003).

Therefore, firms create logistics environmental management as a crucial component of a company's strategic vision that aims to pursue improved environmental and financial results, rather than just as an impromptu operational reaction to external demands (most of the time in a synergetic way).

Bettering one's "competition performance" can signify different things and be done in a variety of ways. The following are the three most popular strategic philosophies that can encourage businesses to embrace GSCM practices:

1. "Reputation-led": By establishing cooperative "green" logistics with providers to reduce transportation emissions and raise awareness of the system among customers and consumers, for instance, the environmental performance of the entire product life cycle can be enhanced. This can dramatically improve a company's reputation;
2. "Efficiency-led": Thanks to creative ideas, a supply chain-focused business strategy can lower the amount of raw materials required to make one unit of the product or lower the weight and thickness of the packaging. Saving money in this way helps the business to offer a product to the market that is competitive in terms of price.
3. "Innovation-led": Another way to look at GSCM is as the outcome of an innovation leader's plan. Pioneering GSCM-related practices present a chance for organizations that are leaders in generating product and process innovations to strengthen their leadership and gain an advantage over their rivals (Vachon and Klassen, 2007).

GSCM techniques can occasionally be seen as a result of a "strategic" process, even if they are not created under one of the aforementioned methodologies. This occurs when "external causes" become so potent that they force followers to adopt GSCM. The widespread adoption of GSCM practices in recent years, particularly in certain industrial sectors (such as food and beverage, textile, and chemicals), has propelled many organizations to adopt the "first-mover" strategy, whereby they work with their suppliers to make up for their marketable disadvantage compared to those who adopted environmental practices first. The latter can be described as an "imitation-led" strategy.

1.5.2 Environmental Management Systems and Sustainable Supply Chains

When examining the determinants of GSCM, additional factors may exist that have a significant impact on a firm's willingness to adopt such practices.

This is particularly true when a company strives for environmental excellence using various tools or solutions that have a strong synergy with (and may recommend the implementation of) GSCM practices. The main findings of the pertinent literature highlight that while early on in an EMS application, ISO 14001-certified or EMAS-registered companies mainly focused on "housekeeping," today these companies are looking "beyond the boundaries" of their production process and organization toward the entire life cycle of their products and services and, consequently, and firstly, to their supply chain.

The extensive use of EMSs in recent years has demonstrated that these "tools" can be useful for managing environmental impacts resulting from supply chain relationships and from the various stages of a product life cycle as well as for the adopter for managing its environmental aspects (Sharfman et al., 1997). A growing number of theoretical and practical studies have discovered that "extending" an EMS using a life cycle approach has considerable promise for "inter-organizational environmental management," i.e., for efficient coordination and cooperation across businesses throughout the supply chain.

This point of view contends that EMSs are essential when a major adopter has to support and involve smaller businesses in its supply chain to meet shared environmental goals. The pertinent material on GSCM stresses that using a supply chain-oriented strategy presents numerous challenges, particularly for SMEs. As a result of its connections and interactions with the other supply chain participants, a company's management control over environmental issues may be insufficient, and its contractual authority within these business relationships may not be sufficient to sway the relevant decision-making (Fuller, 1999).

Gonzalez et al. recently looked into how EMS deployment affected businesses' decisions to "encourage" suppliers to embrace environmental policies (2008). The authors focused on the Spanish automobile industry and discovered a link between the adoption of a certified EMS and the environmental requirements that these businesses place on their suppliers. Additionally, and symmetrically, one of the primary (explicit or contract-based) customer's environmental performance requirements that a company demands of its suppliers is EMS (Simpson and Power, 2005; Simpson et al., 2007).

Since they can be used in tandem (and in a synergistic way), EMS and GSCM practices can be complementary and have positive effects on an organization's environmental performance. This is because they provide a more thorough method for defining and having established sustainable actions among connections of business associates (Darnall et al., 2008a).

1.6 Effects of GSCM on Performance

1.6.1 GSCM as a Managerial Tool for Improving Environmental Performance at the Firm Level

The need for businesses to confront significant environmental obstacles that can't be handled solely by relying on their resources (technical, managerial, or even economic ones) but require the involvement of other actors who are co-responsible for their generation is the main driver behind the increasing diffusion of GSCM. Environmental concerns that cannot be properly answered without the active engagement of suppliers, retailers, clients, and final consumers include the intensive use of raw materials and natural resources, the increasing waste production caused by consumer products and their packaging, and the environmental effects of transporting intermediate and consumer goods to their final markets (Srivastava, 2007). As a result, the primary goal of GSCM and the primary indicator of its success must be its capacity to enhance the environmental performance of the businesses using this strategy as well as of their business partners.

A significant portion of the case study-based research has supported this conclusion. For instance, Geffen and Rothenberg (2000) examined three case studies of US assembly facilities and concluded that strong supplier partnerships, backed by suitable incentive programs, facilitate the acceptance and development of cutting-edge environmental solutions. Furthermore, engagement with suppliers' employees, cooperation agreements, and innovation development all contribute to actual, quantifiable gains in environmental performance as well as the maintenance of product quality and cost targets.

The efficacy of GSCM in enhancing environmental performance is further supported by anecdotal evidence, although relatively few researchers have examined this relationship using quantitative methods based on surveys. In a study on GSCM practices in Chinese manufacturing enterprises, Zhu and Sarkis (2004) examined survey data from 186 respondents and discovered that higher adoption rates of GSCM practices (such as environmental audits for suppliers' internal management, environmental standards for purchased goods, ISO 14001 certification, and collaboration with suppliers and customers for sustainability goals) result in better environmental performance. In addition, a recent study by Iraldo et al. (2009), based on a sample of 100 firms that were interviewed, discovered proof of the impact of a pre-emptive GSCM on environmental performance.

1.6.2 GSCM as a Managerial Tool for Improving Competitive Performance at the Firm Level

The primary incentive for businesses to adopt more environmentally friendly manufacturing practices is the realization of financial gains as "side-effects" of environmental improvement.

According to others, resolving environmental challenges successfully could open up new markets for competitors and inspire creative methods to enhance core corporate operations (Hansmann and Kroger, 2001).

The few empirical studies that have been published that explore the connection between environmental efficiency and competitiveness have almost solely concentrated on commercial performance at the business level. The evidence is not conclusive and unambiguous on this matter; some studies (Jaggi and Freedman, 1992; Hamilton, 1995) revealed a weak or statistically insignificant relationship between economic and environmental performance, but more recent studies came to the opposite result (Iraldo et al., 2009). For example, Al-Tuwaijiri et al. (2004) show that strong environmental performance is substantially associated with good commercial success through the use of a simultaneous equation model.

Numerous experts agree that a management strategy focused on the supply chain can have considerable economic as well as environmental benefits. Inter-firm relationships, according to Dodgson (2000) and Dyer and Singh (1998), offer formal and informal methods that foster trust, lower risk, and ultimately boost innovation and profitability. Involvement, analysis, and control mechanisms along the supply chain based on environmental criteria are some of the important components of GSCM that can lower the risks of delivery delays or interruptions brought on by a crucial supplier's compliance issue (Lipman, 1999).

The South-East Asia Region, where GSCM use appears to be more widespread, has received the majority of attention in this empirical research emphasizing the competitive consequences of GSCM adoption. For instance, the work by Zhu and Sarkis (2004) cited above, which examines GSCM practice in Chinese manufacturing firms, demonstrated that businesses that create a lot of GSCM practices perform better in the competitive market. Finally, Rao and Holt's investigation from 2005 discovered that "greening" the various supply chain phases results in a more integrated and cooperative supply chain, which eventually boosts competitiveness.

1.7 Supply Chain Performance Measurement

1.7.1 Supply Chain Management

The administration of a complicated network of operations involved in getting a finished product to the consumer or end user is known as supply chain management. It is a crucial business activity, and the procedure entails obtaining raw materials and components, producing and putting together goods, storing them, entering and tracking orders, distributing them through various channels, and eventually delivering them to the consumer. Customers, internal company processes, outside distributors, and external suppliers make up a company's supply chain structure (commercial or end-user). Companies may participate in several supply chains at once. The administration and coordination are made more difficult by the worldwide nature of the actors, who operate across time zones and geographical boundaries. Customer expectations, globalization, information technology, governmental regulations, competition, and the environment all have an impact on how successfully a supply chain is managed.

1.7.2 Performance Management and Measurement

Qualitative and quantitative measurements and methods are both used in corporate performance measurement, which is still expanding. The organization's aim or the unique characteristics of each strategic business unit have a significant impact on the range and intensity of performance measures. For instance, organizations must evaluate performance using more strategic and competitive financial measures including rate of return, profits, customer base, and sales volumes. Some measurements, such as consumer happiness and warehouse efficiency (turnover, supply), are mainly administratively focused but could also be connected to measures and issues at the strategic level.

In general, the numerous measurement taxonomies are to blame for these challenges in creating standards for performance measurement. Examples of taxonomic factors are the management level to measure—strategic, tactical, or operational—tangible versus intangible metrics, variances in data gathering and reporting, the organization's position along the supply chain, or functional differentiation within organizations (e.g. accounting versus marketing or operations).

Similar to how performance is measured, each organization or unit within an organization may have its specific performance measurement system that reflects both the environment and the organization's primary goals. Numerous researchers have looked into the fundamentals of measuring performance (Adams et al., 1995; Gunasekaran et al., 2001; Sink and Tuttle, 1990). These studies came to several conclusions about performance measurement and its systems, such as systems and indicators are best utilized with a cooperative effort with derivation from and links to corporate strategy; measures should be adaptable and present at multiple levels; products and procedures need to be included; and measures are best developed with a balance of both types of measures.; Systems must be capable of connecting compensation, incentives, and recognition to performance measurement; accountability for results must be assigned and understood; systems need to provide intelligence for decision-makers rather than just compile data; and systems must have efficient internal and external communications. It has also been stated that performance measurement must shift into performance management, where the organization creates the proper organizational structure and has the capability of utilizing the results of performance measurement to effect change inside the organization.

Performance measurement is crucial to any business in managing its operations, and it is at the heart of comprehensive quality as well as continuous improvement projects. There are several applications for performance measurement, including assessing the efficacy and efficiency of an existing system or contrasting competing alternative systems. Typically, suggested systems are planned, designed, implemented, and monitored through performance measurement.

1.7.3 Linking the Supply Chain and Performance Measurement

The importance placed on logistics performance measurement (especially with an inter-organizational emphasis), either in the practitioner or research community, has been relatively limited, despite significant work having been done on performance measurement and management of internal organizational operations (Gunasekaran et al., 2004).

The focus of supply chain models has typically been on performance metrics like cost (Cohen and Lee, 1989; Cohen and Moon, 1990; Lee and Feitzinger, 1995; Tzafestas and Kapsiotis, 1994), as well as a blend of cost and user responsiveness (Arntzen et al., 1995; Altiok and Ranjan, 1995; Cook and Rogowski, 1996; Davis, 1993; Towill et al., 1992; Wikner et al., 1991; Lee and Billington, 1993; Christopher, 1994; Nicoll, 1994).

Some of the available research does offer preliminary insights on measuring the performance of a wider supply chain. Evaluation of supplier performance and research into acceptable performance metrics have received special focus (Davis, 1993; Nicoll, 1994; Carr and Pearson, 1999; Carr and Smeltzer, 1997, 1999; Chen and Paulraj, 2002). The majority of this research has also concentrated on creating and analyzing supplier performance assessment constructs and the functions they serve.

Beamon and Chen (2001), building on previous research, look at the effects of several factors on logistics performance and describe the relationship that exists between these components and overall supply network performance. They found that the likelihood function of demand, the overall inventory stock-out risk, and the transit time had the biggest roles in determining how effective the chain was (Beamon and Chen, 2001).

An overview of the numerous performance measures used throughout the supply chain is given by Gunasekaran et al. (2001), along with a description of the sources that use them. They examine the plan, acquire, make/assemble, and deliver operations of a single organization's supply chain in an integrative model and offer metrics suitable for managing these four "fundamental links" of the supply chain. They did acknowledge the need for additional research on these generic indicators, but they did not include measurements that were specifically focused on the environment (Gunasekaran et al., 2001).

Gunasekaran et al. (2004) offer insights into present practice and future needs in supply chain performance measurement, covering topics pertinent to our discussion on GSCM/PM later on. This is a more recent empirical study. These problems include: organization-wide coordination is necessary for successful implementation; each metric for performance monitoring must take a supply chain perspective; each supply chain entity should be measured and improved with shared objectives; non-financial metrics are receiving more attention than financial ones; and additional and innovative efforts are required to design new measures (Gunasekaran et al., 2004).

Brewer and Speh (2001) raise several issues with the use of systems and tools for performance monitoring throughout the supply chain, such as the following:

a. Dispelling mistrust: Practices in traditional SCM have been competitive. Building trust in data sharing, collection, and monitoring is necessary.

b. A lack of comprehension: Managers that are primarily concerned with internal systems find it challenging to comprehend multi-organizational measurements.

c. A lack of command: Organizations and managers want to be judged on factors they can influence. Inter-organizational actions are challenging to oversee and subsequently control.

d. Distinctive purposes and aims: Various organizations would advocate for distinct measures because they have different purposes.

e. Information technology: The majority of enterprise information systems are unable to collect non-traditional data on supply chain performance.

f. The absence of uniform performance metrics: There might not be any agreed-upon standards for the usage of units, organization, format, etc.

g. The challenge of connecting metrics to consumer value: The relationship between stakeholder value and environmental challenges is growing increasingly complicated. It is also unclear how a supply chain defines the term "client."

h. Selecting a starting point: It is challenging to develop supply chain-wide performance since boundaries aren't always obvious.

Strong leadership, communication, and cooperation initiatives across firms can help overcome these obstacles, but it's obvious that more organizations need to take a cooperative position.

1.8 Green Supply Chain Management in Developed Countries

According to Srivastava's definition of GSCM in 2007, this includes product design, material sourcing and selection, production methods, delivering finished goods to customers, and managing products' end-of-life after their useful lives. Green design, environmental sourcing/procurement, ecological operations or manufacturing, green distribution, green logistics/marketing, and resource- efficient logistics are all included in GSCM (Srivastava, 2007).

Compared to emerging or non-developed economies, the genesis and wide distribution of GSCM are more frequently linked to developed economies. High levels of industrialization, economic growth, and the Human Development Index define developed nations. In industrialized nations, several scholars undertook studies to look at how supply chain management and environmental concepts could be combined. Five potential drivers of GSCM performance were identified in a study from Germany by Large and Thomsen (2011). These drivers included Green Supply Management capabilities, the strategic level of the purchasing department, the level of environmental commitment, the degree of green supplier assessment, and the degree of green collaboration with suppliers. In the context of the Portuguese automotive supply chain, Azevedo et al. (2011) looked at the connections between sustainable practices found in a distribution network and the effect they have on that chain's effectiveness. Compared to emerging or non-developed economies, the genesis and wide distribution of GSCM are more frequently linked to developed economies. High levels of industrialization, economic growth, and the Human Development Index define developed nations. In industrialized nations, many scholars undertook studies to look at how supply chain management and environmental concepts could be combined. Five major drivers of GSCM performance were identified in a study from Germany by Large and Thomsen (2011). These drivers included Green Supply Management capabilities, the strategic level of the purchasing department, the level of environmental commitment, the degree of green supplier assessment, and the degree of green partnership with suppliers. These programs assist in assessing the environmental performance of suppliers and require them to follow particular environmental norms. In a different Japanese study, Zhu et al. (2010) aimed to present the sustainability and GSCM practices of significant Japanese manufacturers. The study showed that by going green the distribution networks and developing bonus connections with their partners, global corporations may achieve sustainable growth across their supplier networks. Additionally, it shows how effective government rules and policies can promote the transfer of GSCM from bigger, more established enterprises to smaller ones.

By using factor analysis, Hsu and Hu (2008) looked at the consistency techniques that affect GSCM adoption and implementation in the Taiwanese electronics industry. Nine companies in the electronic industry used the fuzzy analytic hierarchy process method to rank the relative relevance of four dimensions and 20 approaches. Meanwhile, Shang et al. (2010) investigated major GSCM capability dimensions and firm performance using Taiwanese manufacturing companies that produced electronics. Six GSCM dimensions—green manufacturing and packaging, green marketing, green suppliers, green stock, and green eco-design—were discovered by factor analysis. The extent and type of greening of the supply chain in the UK manufacturing sector were explored by Holt and Ghobadian (2009). This study looks at the reasons underlying environmental management, the specific behaviors that come as a result, and the relationships between them. The Nawrocka et al. study (2009) The application of ISO 14001 in Swedish businesses' environmental supply management practices has received a lot of attention in Sweden. To communicate the requirements to the supplier, inspire and enable the supplier, and ensure that the supplier complies with the requirements, the study described the current and potential roles of ISO 14001 for these three crucial operational tasks of environmental supply chain management. To ascertain what drives small and medium-sized suppliers to participate in GSC programs, Lee (2008) looked at these businesses' most important stakeholders, including consumers and the government. In 2008, Raymond et al. looked at the connection between supply chains and the environmental performance of Small and Medium-sized Enterprises (SMEs) in Canada. This investigation showed that the biggest constraining factors for addressing solid waste and energy concerns are time and financial resources. Chen (2008) also investigated the connection between green innovation and Taiwanese enterprises' perceptions of being environmentally friendly. The study put out the idea of a new Green Core Competence. Chien and Shih (2007) looked at how the Taiwanese electrical and electronic industries adopted GSCM practices. Studies have been done on how GSCM procedures affect both financial and environmental performance. One Australian study, done by Simpson et al. (2007), looked at the effectiveness of the customer's environmental performance requirements as well as the moderating effect of the relationship circumstances that exist between a customer and its suppliers. Almost no study has been done on how successful green supply requirements are in reality, taking inter-organizational dynamics into account.

1.9 Green Supply Chain Management in Underdeveloped Nations

Many people believe that GSCM reflects the ideal of environmentally friendly systems, technologies, processes, products, and business practices. GSCM is often thought to reflect the image of environmentally friendly products, processes, systems, technology, and business conduct. Instead of taking a proactive stance to limit the sources of waste or pollution, the majority of businesses, particularly in developing nations, implemented green solutions into their operations to lessen the adverse effects on the environment. The classic "command-and-control" or "end-of-the-pipe" solutions continue to be these adopted green solutions (Anbumozhi and Kanada, 2005). The concern of GSCM in developing nations has not received adequate attention in the literature. Only a few businesses in the South East Asian region are likely to be able to apply the GSCM concept because it is a relatively new idea (Rao, 2002). According to Rao (2002) in his investigation of the green supply chain in the South East Asian Region, GSCM practices have started to take root. As a result, the research findings from the Asian region can be applied to manufacturing in emerging nations to assist create the best GSCM methods and lessen environmental issues. Recent literature revealed that some academics have begun examining the growth of GSCM in the East Asian region, including China, which is known for having complex GSCM difficulties because it is a significant manufacturing nation. Zhu et al. (2011) looked at whether or not the degree to which various Chinese manufacturer clusters apply GSCM differs from an ecological modernization standpoint. The study also looked at how well-aware Chinese manufacturers were of regional and global environmental regulations connected to the implementation of GSCM that were ESPR-oriented (improving energy savings and pollution reduction). Additionally, he concluded that the mediating impact of regulatory pressure is a significant factor in the adoption of GSCM procedures. It is argued that the adoption of GSCM methods by the Chinese manufacturing industry has progressed at different rates among Chinese manufacturers, highlighting the importance of regulatory pressure. The link between the identified determinant factors and the GSCM level has been examined in the study by Liu et al. (2011) in China. The study indicated that regular internal training of employees to expand a company's involvement in GSCM procedures will significantly improve a company's environmental management capabilities. Yan Li (2011) investigated a different piece of Chinese research that looked at GSCM adoption rates as well as GSCM performance measurement. The results showed that

GSCM significantly balanced other advanced management methods and enhanced environmental performance. Zhu et al. (2008) looked at GSCM practices related to closing the supply chain loop for four Chinese industries: power generation, chemical and petroleum, electrical and electronics, and autos. They concluded that there are differences in how the four industries use GSCM practices in various industrial scenarios. In a separate study conducted in China by Zhu et al. in 2005, the GSCM drivers' practices, and performance of various Chinese manufacturing enterprises were assessed and explained. Researchers' interest in examining the development and use of GSCM methods in other Asian nations including Thailand, India, and Malaysia has increased due to concerns about environmental difficulties. In a study conducted in Thailand by Ninlawan et al. (2011), the level of GSCM was examined in addition to current green initiatives in computer parts manufacturers being analyzed. A thorough interview has been done addressing green manufacturing, green distribution, and green reverse logistics. By using an Interpretive Structural Modelling 892 JMTM 26,6 Downloaded by Indian Institute of Technology RoorkeeAt 01:57 05 August 2015 (PT) methodology, Diabat and Govindan (2011)'s study in India extracted 11 drivers from the literature to identify the factors influencing the implementation of GSCM.Regulations, customer requirements, anticipated economic profits, and social responsibility are the four main reasons or motivators for GSC activities, according to a Malaysian study by Eltayeb and Zailani (2009). Eltayeb et al. (2011) examined the relationship between GSC efforts and performance results and identified the primary initiatives (eco-design) that have a favorable impact on the four types of outcomes (environmental, economic, cost reductions, and intangible outcomes).

1.10 Green Supply Chain Management in India

Over 50% of all pollution produced in India is attributable to industrial waste. 17 industries have been identified by the government as severely polluting, while 24 have been identified as having environmental issues. The bulk of industrial pollution in the nation is produced by the chemical and engineering industries, which are the main offenders. Integrated iron and steel plants, non-ferrous metallurgical units, pharmaceutical and petrochemical complexes, fertilizer and pesticide production facilities, thermal power plants, textile, pulp and paper, tannery, and chloralkali units are a few additional well-known sectors. A rough estimate of 70% of the total industrial pollution produced countrywide in 2006 came from SMEs, which made up 40% of the industrial production and only used basic pollution control technology (OECD Report, 2006).

It should come as no surprise that the world's fifth-largest emitter of Green House Gases (GHG) is the fourth-largest economy in the world. India's carbon dioxide emissions climbed more than 1.5 times between 1990 and 2008, making them the second-highest in the world behind China. Rapid industrialization is depleting resources and producing four million tonnes of garbage, which is a significant amount. Only 3% of e-waste, which is by itself in the hazardous category, gets recycled at permitted recycling facilities. The industrial sector in India must quickly implement GSCM measures due to the existing levels of pollution and waste (Bhattacharya et al., 2011).

India is the country where implementing GSCP is most relevant. The manufacturing industry, which currently accounts for 16% of the GDP, is expected to develop and, as a result of the SME sector, will contribute 25% more to GDP growth by 2022. Efficiency-wise, the SME sector's performance is not particularly encouraging. For SMEs, issues include rising input costs, such as energy costs, a lack of resources (especially power, fossil fuels, etc.), poor logistics management, and a lack of skilled labour. Cost reductions through the greening of supply chains in the SME sector must now more than ever be addressed seriously in India to combat these. The Indian SME landscape is known for its unwillingness to abandon old traditions, which significantly hinders the adoption of GSCM measures. The tendency also applies to larger business structures. Knowledge of green technologies, practices, and methodologies, when combined with willingness, is essential for making the supply chain green. The top management has a significant lack of expertise, which is preventing the spread of GSCM in India (TERI, 2013).

Aside from SMEs, the other area of concentration is agriculture, which cannot be overlooked because it is essential to India's socioeconomic structure. In India, agriculture is a significant energy consumer, and understanding renewable energy technology can significantly aid the industry in going green. Modern irrigation techniques like sprinklers, drip, and micro-irrigation are essential for lowering the amount of water needed for irrigation as well as the amount of electricity or diesel needed to power the pump sets. In India, sales of motors are primarily made up of inefficient motors. Retrofitting even only 10% of the existing, ineffective pump sets (15.35 million as of March 2007) may save users 4 billion kWh (kilowatt-hours) annually and add 900 MW of equivalent generation capacity. Along the same line, efforts must be taken to manage crop residue, fertilizers, irrigation water, precision agriculture, pesticide control, etc. in an environmentally sustainable manner (Govindan and Bhanot, 2012). The "National Mission on Sustainable Agriculture" calls for efforts to assure better livestock, crop seeds, and fish culture, as well as better pest management, farming practices, nutrient management, and increased water efficiency. Additionally, it urges the creation of new market infrastructure, the synchronization of R&D with market demands, and the diversification of sources of income (NMSA Report, 2010).

On a more positive note, due to the advantages it offers in terms of better efficiency, several parts of the Indian SME sector have taken the initiative in implementing GSCM procedures. Manufacturers of cutting and hand tools, automobile parts, spare parts, industrial equipment, and machinery, among others, appear to be relatively advanced in their use of green storage and distribution strategies. However, rather than being the norm, these occurrences are more of an exception. India's Environmental Performance Index (EPI) ranking in 2012 was a pitiful 125 out of 132 nations. Instead of focusing on policy inputs like program budget expenditures or policy outputs like emissions or deforestation rates, EPI analyses the efficiency of national environmental protection activities. India's low ranking reveals the deplorable state of its knowledge of GSCM practices (Nimawat and Namdev, 2012). Despite this, it is possible to say that environmental awareness is growing across many Indian supply chain players if it is not yet maximally significant. Organic food, solar heaters, electrical autos, and other "Green Products" are becoming more and more popular among Indian customers and businesses. Indian manufacturing is catching up to the long-term advantages of environmentally friendly procedures to enhance business brands, cut costs, and satisfy compliance all at once. Lean processes are being implemented by energy-intensive businesses to reduce waste and improve energy efficiency (CII, 2011). Even though more businesses are using GSCM in India, it is safe to say that there is still little broad knowledge of the idea among suppliers, customers, and staff. The idea of RL, where waste may be reclaimed from the customer and reused or disposed of in an environmentally sustainable manner, is also lacking in the majority of businesses (Dutta and Vaibhavanand, 2012).

The Indian government is concerned about implementing regulations that can stop environmental deterioration because it recognizes the value of environmentally friendly industrial practices and the benefits that result from them. According to the Planning Commission of India's Manufacturing Plan, producers should not view being green as a requirement, but rather as a commercial priority. On the other hand, the government must create institutional assistance for micro, small, and medium-sized businesses (MSMEs), as they will find it difficult to meet standards because of their inadequate and obsolete technology.

In his study, Sarkis (2011) noted that there are several opportunities for researchers to uncover new elements of the GSCM concept because so many of its potential facets have yet to be discovered. In addition, a large portion of the literature on the topic is recent, indicating that the idea is still in its infancy and that additional surprises will emerge as our understanding of the topic advances toward its development and maturity. Sarkis stated his claim from a broader perspective. According to Sarkis, GSCM has produced significant gains for the employing firms—both economic and environmental—despite being in its infancy even in the Western world. Given that the percolation of GSCM, even in its current stage of infancy, has been limited, the benefits awaiting developing nations like India are vast. This not only presents opportunities, but also problems in the form of knowledge and information transmission, as well as building the necessary capacities to reach its threshold level of acceptability, adoption, and execution.

In 2005, the biggest retailer in the world unveiled a comprehensive company sustainability strategy. Wal-Mart, a giant in the retail sector, had a serious issue with packaging waste. It was determined that a 5% reduction in packing may prevent the atmospheric release of around 6.5 metric tonnes of carbon dioxide and generate savings of almost $10 billion. The business decided to put the strategy into action and benefited from it.

A lot of MNCs are aiming for "zero trash for disposal." The same objective is being pursued by this international food and beverage corporation from Switzerland. Through the effective use of water disposal systems, Nestlé, the firm under consideration, attempts to address issues relating to rural communities, and the safety of soil, water, and air. Nestle's sustainability initiatives allowed for zero trash to be generated at around 35 of its factories in 2012.

"Aware of Energy" is a program that Heineken has put in place. The company educates its staff about energy issues through this program. The business prioritizes energy efficiency, the utilization of renewable resources, etc. For every hectolitre of beer produced, the company has saved 17% of its energy. Additionally, it wants to cut its installed fridge base's carbon footprint by 50% by the year 2020.

Regarding the adjacent nation, China, the third-largest economy in the world, there is a significant problem with tonnes of solid garbage. The nation's ability to convert garbage into electricity has advanced significantly (WTE). China has increased its WTE capacity from 2 million tonnes to 14 million tonnes, making it the fourth-largest consumer of WTE. In 2007, there were 66 WTE plants, and there are now more than 100, according to estimates. China has been able to do this and produce $30 per MWH of electricity.

The International Renewable Energy Agency has picked a city in the center of Abu Dhabi as its headquarters (IRENA). The development of Masdar City, which will be powered by renewable energy, has cost $22 billion. There will be more than 1500 businesses in the city. Their primary goals will be to support research and development initiatives and contribute to the creation of innovative, sustainable technology. There will be no cars allowed to drive in this metropolis, which will also have zero garbage, and a solar-powered desalination facility will assist supply water to the entire city. Saudi Arabia is positioned to overtake China as the world's top exporter of solar energy due to its extensive open spaces and exposure to sunlight.

The topic of sustainability has received a lot of attention and is now being discussed in board meetings. Global warming has become a significant concern as a result of rising energy use and population. Companies have begun branding their internal initiatives to foster an environmentally friendly atmosphere (e.g. P&G, PepsiCo, Cadbury, Coca-Cola – refer to Fig.)

Some Indian businesses are implementing green supply chain management, learning from overseas businesses in the process. The graph below shows the advancements made by India in terms of environmental and sustainability issues:

1.10.1 ITC

ITC is a business organization with a wide range of ventures, including FMCG, hotels, paper and packaging, agro, and more. It is a member of the prestigious Forbes 2000 list and has an annual revenue of roughly $8 billion. The business is setting the bar high for numerous green efforts, including the adoption of ECF (Elemental Chlorine Free) technology, ozone bleaching, energy and water management strategies, and most recently, the introduction of a green boiler mechanism. The corporation can cut its reliance on fossil fuels like coal by over 100,000 tonnes annually by putting the aforementioned green strategies into practice. ITC has benefited from the recycling of waste materials in the production of paperboards for packaging. ITC has created a sizable advantage in raw material sustainability through the usage of e-choupals, and as a result, is profiting from it. As a result, the organization has emerged as a leader in green management efforts and is dedicated to lowering carbon footprints.

1.10.2 Dr Reddy's

Consumers and regulators in India are putting a lot of pressure on the pharmaceutical business to lessen its impact on the environment. In this situation, pharmaceutical companies' supply chains have come under intense scrutiny. One such business that prioritizes sustainable sourcing is Dr. Reddy's. They have started a mentoring process in which they communicate with all of their business partners and advise them on how to adopt sustainable business practices. The business emphasizes regular quality training for all of its vendors, especially for those who are new business partners. These half- yearly events assist the corporation in communicating its business practices and culture to all of its partners.

1.10.3 L&T

An engineering and construction firm with a yearly revenue of roughly $14 billion in Larsen & Toubro Limited (L&T). The corporation is heavily involved in industries such as heavy engineering, infotech, hydrocarbons, and construction. The company is the first in India to begin reporting on sustainability. The 3R principle—reduce, recycle, and reuse—has been applied by the corporation in a number of its efforts. L&T can collect more than 23 million gallons of rainwater as a result. Water use has decreased by 6% overall, and there has been no wastewater discharge on 16 campuses. Infrastructure-wise, they have constructed energy-efficient buildings and heavily utilize renewable energies like wind and solar electricity throughout their premises. The business incorporates recycled materials like fly ash and crushed sand into its raw material needs. The business frequently engages stakeholders (internal and external) to pinpoint important material challenges. To reduce staff travel and subsequently the use of cars, the organization also promotes the use of video conferencing for internal meetings.

1.10.4 TCS

TCS is using Environmentally friendly materials. TCS has boosted the use of renewable energy in its offices, starting with the infrastructure. According to data from 2012–2013, the solar water capacity is around 86,600 liters per day, which is an increase of 55% from the figures from the prior year. The business is also emphasizing green supplier procurement. It has placed a focus on buying energy star-certified equipment. The business has started several campaigns and internal communications among its staff about the advantages of energy conservation. Basic actions include turning off computers at the end of the day and using fewer lights for more complex ones like installing variable frequency drives. TCS can cut the usage of freshwater by almost 13% compared to 2008 figures by using rainwater collecting, sewage treatment facilities, and other water management strategies. E-waste is a problem that all IT majors must contend with daily. The

government-approved recyclers are used to legally dispose of outdated/defunct computers. To lessen employee travel to client locations by car and lower greenhouse gas emissions, video conferencing is promoted throughout all TCS facilities.

1.10.5 State Bank of India

Paperless banking has taken on a new dimension thanks to SBI Bank's ground-breaking effort known as "Green Channel Counter." Without filling out any physical documents, an account holder can transfer funds, withdraw money, and even deposit money into another account. All of these purchases can be done with a single card swipe. The bank has also introduced solar-powered ATMs in rural regions, which not only help them increase their customer base but also use 1000 watts less power than traditional ATMs.

1.10.6 Oil and Natural Gas Company (ONGC)

The largest oil company in India, ONGC, has teamed up with the Mokshda Paryavaran Evam Van Suraksha Samiti to create a green cremation that is energy-efficient. This will alter the current burning mechanism. The innovative idea will considerably reduce air and water pollution while also assisting in a 60% reduction in wood consumption.

1.11 Need for Green SCM –Opportunity for Organisations

India has already developed into one of the largest economies in the world and is a prestigious member of the trillion-dollar club. Both the rural and urban sectors will continue to see tremendous growth. In this scenario, the environment and ecology have been severely impacted by the rise in energy demand and consumption, the rise in greenhouse gas emissions, and the scarcity of vital natural resources including land, water, and oil. These problems require immediate attention and priority treatment. Consumers in India are becoming more and more interested in environmental preservation. Consumers in today's technologically advanced society are more aware of and engaged with ecological issues, and as a result, they are adapting their behavior to fit a socially responsible lifestyle. Going green can help businesses make long-term profits while simultaneously saving the environment and reducing their influence on it. Additionally, the media generates beneficial attention for the businesses that carry out green efforts. Positive media attention for going green can improve the company's reputation greatly. Therefore, businesses that actively participate in going green will become more visible and credible. By implementing a green initiative program, businesses can be certain that they will abide by all current and upcoming environmental laws and regulations. As a result of the depletion of raw materials, degradation of the environment, overpopulation of wastelands, and rising pollution levels, green supply chain management (GSCM) is becoming more and more important. It's important to be environmentally friendly in today's competitive market in addition to having greater business sense and profitability.

Organizations can benefit from green SCM in the following manner:-

1. Savings:

The green movement offers chances for long-term savings. Companies must demonstrate their long-term commitment by sticking with the GSCM investment. They might eventually achieve a period of revenue neutrality, at least in the medium run. Although the corporation shouldn't anticipate seeing significant benefits right away from using Green SCM, it can undoubtedly assert itself as a competitive advantage for businesses offering products with environmental qualities.

2. Lower risk:

Companies can minimize risks that frequently result in expenses or losses by purchasing greener goods or services. There are numerous instances where vendors and suppliers of a corporation use illicit methods to obtain or sell raw materials, harming the company's reputation. Several of the supplier villages have a really bad history with the environment. By employing and abiding by environmentally friendly techniques, these hazards can be reduced.

3. Increase in revenue:

By leveraging tools like green supply-chain management, businesses are striving to increase the effectiveness of their business processes and decrease the use of energy and materials. As a result of the industry's leading investment in energy efficiency, renewable energy, and green construction projects, stakeholder demands have been met, brand reputation has improved, and consumer loyalty has increased.

4. Indirect yield:-

Being environmentally friendly allows an organization to significantly cut waste while also protecting the environment. It can improve the company's brand image and will inadvertently raise employee, supplier, and other stakeholder motivation levels.

1.12 Challenges

It's challenging to implement GSCM. Organizations will likely encounter a variety of difficulties, some of which include:

i. Cost is cited as the largest obstacle to implementing green supply chain management.

ii. Businesses often adopt any new technology or process when they can quantify the results. However, because GSCM is a simplistic idea, it has become more challenging to use any quantifiable data to evaluate the efficacy of the value chain.

iii. A suitable technology must be in place to support businesses with green practices.

iv. A lack of green contractors, developers, consultants, and architects in the area. The organizations are reluctant to proceed with the investment because there aren't enough green practitioners accessible.

v. Integrating product recycling is a crucial component of GSCM. The integration of trash (recycling) as raw materials to be utilized once again in production units is a significant problem for many businesses.

vi. The dread of failing is another difficulty. The organizations lack confidence in the likelihood that the green program will succeed or fail miserably.

vii. A lack of knowledge about the best practices, rules, and implementation procedures.

viii. The top-level management's support and dedication are essential for the successful implementation of a GSCM program, but sadly owing to a lack of faith in the idea and hefty initial costs, the top management is reluctant to apply green practices.

ix. Because there are numerous stakeholders involved in the supply chain, anyone's unwillingness to accept and participate in the design process and technology has an impact on the chain's performance as a whole.

x. Finally, because consumers are unaware of GSCM and green products, businesses are reluctant to implement them.

The three categories of distribution planning issues include distribution allocation, location-allocation, and vehicle routing issues. These issues can be combined with other supply chain issues to create new, practical supply chain concepts that can be used to address problems in the real world (Novitasari, M., &Agustia, D., 2021). For instance, the location-routing problem is an operational- strategic issue that arises from merging vehicle routing and location issues in many chains, including plastics manufacturing, healthcare, and hazardous waste management (Rabbani et al. 2018) and plastic (Qazvini et al. 2019). Another issue that has drawn more attention in the literature recently is the combination of location-routing problems with inventory control issues (Gholipour et al. 2020; Saif-Eddine et al. 2019; Rafie-Majd et al. 2018).

CHAPTER-2

Literature Review

2.1 Overview

A critical aspect of academic research is conducting a thorough review of previous literature. A comprehensive literature review sets the groundwork for future research, highlights areas in need of further study, and aids in generating new hypotheses (Jane, 2002). As awareness grows among businesses and academia regarding the importance of managing environmental projects beyond corporate boundaries, the literature on Green Supply Chain Management (GSCM) is expanding. Recent articles have explored the relationship between corporate environmental management and its operations, demonstrating the need for GSCM research (Liu, Yang; Srai, Jagjit Singh; Evans, Steve, 2016; Stranieri, Stefanella; Varacca, Alessandro; Casati, Mirta; Capri, Ettore; Soregaroli, Claudio, 2022). Industrial ecosystems, extended producer responsibility, product stewardship, product life cycle analysis, and industrial ecology are some of the inter-organizational environmental problems that GSCM is closely linked with. The growing literature on sustainability and ethics, which covers various social and economic factors, also includes GSCM. As a result, "triple-bottom-line" research is on the rise. GSCM research addresses various topics, such as organizational research and practice, GSCM practices, and technology evaluation prescriptive models (AdebaTickle, Matthew, 2013; Beske, Philip; Seuring, Stefan, 2014). Here researcher has analyzed different aspects of the green supply chain through a thorough literature review. The literature review mentioned in this chapter is done as per the below-mentioned three-stage process.

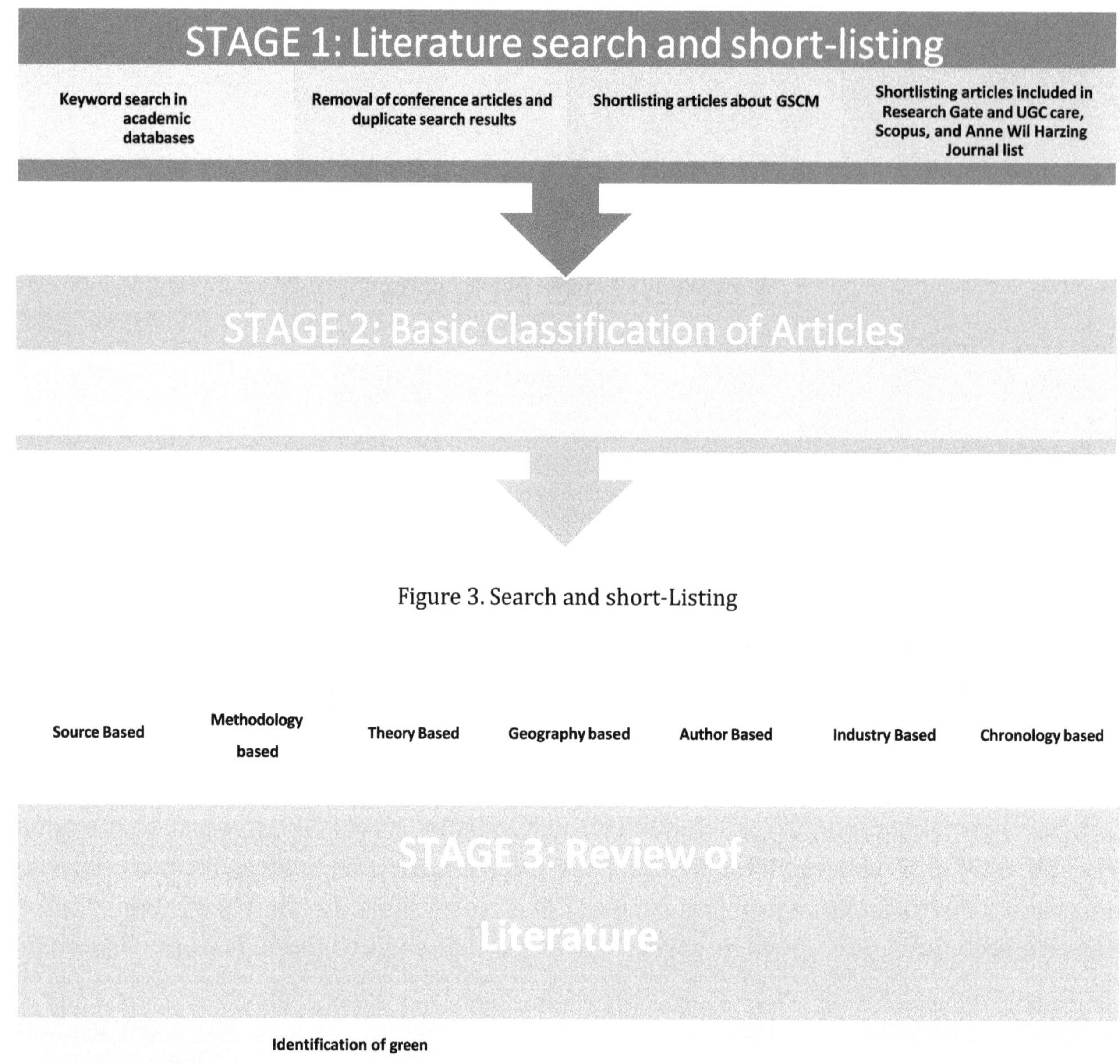

Figure 3. Search and short-Listing

2.2 Key Facts Related to Green Supply Chain Practices

Key Facts Related to Green Supply Chain Practices	Authors
1. The most effective way to use GSCM techniques is in tandem. Therefore, managers should treat investments in internal and external GSCM practices equally. Improvement in Environment Performance is the main objective of GSCM implementation	Luc Muyldermansb,* Katri Kauppi (2015)
2. GSCM more depend upon the customer factor and can be influenced by small firms rather than large companies	Gabriela Scur, Mayara Emília Barbosa (2016)

Key Facts Related to Green Supply Chain Practices	Authors
3. In GSCM economic performance has had the Strongest relationship factor that impacts the working of GSCM on theother hand Social factors have weaker factors identified.	Ruoqi Geng (2017)
4. GSCM can be implemented for manufacturing eco- friendly product industry and ability to sustain in the industry and awareness about the green economy	Kannan Govindan (2013)
5. Enterprise green management improves financial performance while also moderating the indirect impact of supply chain relationships on financial performance. The findings add to the body of knowledge on relationship capital and green management by elaborating on the meaning of relationships in the supply chain and enhancing the application of green management.	Yubing Yu a (2022), Justin Zuopeng Zhang (2022)
6. implement an SSCM to safeguard the interests of future generations from environmental harm. Companies with greener supply chains are getting ready for long-term benefits. With improved sales and social acceptance in the eyes of the client, sustainable businesses would be able to stand out from their rivals.	MdTanvirSira (2023)
7. Corporate value promotion, organizational system and management technology, and corporation with outside parties are all discovered to be key predictors of corporate performance. Internal organizational activity has the biggest impact on operational performance and fosters corporate value and corporation with the outside for foreign-owned vehicle businesses with sophisticated green concepts.	Xintao Li Diyi Liu (2022)
8. Organizational environment performance and green evolution are the two major pillars in the GSCM domain to survive in a competitive industry	Neeraj Lamba, Priyavrat Thareja (2020)
9. Significant cost increases result in rising operational and investment costs, which are bad for business. Manufacturers must understand, though, that making investments in buying environmentally friendly raw materials can assist manage environmental effects, waste management, and energy consumption costs more affordably. Additionally, it is crucial to emphasize firmly the components of internal business operations.	Ru-Jen LinRong-Huei Chen(2011)
10. Managers in developing market firms should place more emphasis on technical practices and less on behavioral-oriented GSCM practices.	Junjun Liua (2022), Houbao Hub (2020)

2.3 Supply Chain Practices in Industry 5.0

The integration of environmental thinking in supply chains led to the emergence of Green Supply Chain Management (GSCM), which encompasses various aspects, including product design, material sourcing, manufacturing techniques, customer distribution, and end-of-life management (Srivastava, 2007). Over the years, supply chains have evolved from simple customer-supplier relationships to strategic partnerships involving shared information.

Environmental issues are now a crucial consideration for the entire network of suppliers within the supply chain (Centobelli, P.; Cerchione, R.; Esposito, 2018). To reduce carbon emissions and promote sustainability, supply chains are implementing renewable energy sources, reducing energy use, and promoting material recycling. Closed-loop supply chain approaches emphasize the importance of material recycling, which can increase revenue while reducing carbon emissions. Supply chain management is not a new concept, as it dates back to ancient trade routes, military logistics, and industrial businesses. Jay W. Forrester is credited with developing modern-day SCM by highlighting the importance of flows of information, material, personnel, equipment, and money in determining industrial business performance (Sahu, Srichandan; Rao, KVSS Narayana, 2021).

Supply chain disruptions can lead to financial challenges for companies. However, existing studies that examine the financial impact of these disruptions have mostly concentrated on large companies in developed economies. Furthermore, there is a lack of substantial contributions that estimate the magnitude of different supply chain disruptions. To bridge this gap, a recent study investigated the effect of supply chain disruptions on the shareholders of small and mid-cap businesses in India (Alora, Aswin; Barua, Mukesh Kumar, 2021).

Research on supply chain risk management has primarily focused on conceptual areas such as planning, mitigation, and disruption management. However, there has been less emphasis on measuring the actual effects of these disruptions (Filbeck et al., 2016). An event study approach revealed that supply chain interruptions resulted in a 1.94% reduction in shareholder wealth. Additionally, the study compared supply-side disruptions to catastrophic and infrastructure catastrophes and found that regulatory concerns had a more significant negative impact. However, this research was conducted in the United States and did not consider financial disruptions or small businesses (Van Wassenhove and Akkermans 2018).

Applying effective and efficient supply chain management practices among partners can offer several opportunities for Indian manufacturers, especially Small and Medium Enterprises (SMEs), to achieve strategic competitiveness over their rivals (Chikan, 2008). Proper SCM practices are vital for enhancing overall organizational performance. Therefore, businesses aim to improve their strategic competitiveness and performance by applying appropriate SCM practices (Chandak, Amit; Kumar, Neeraj; Dalpati, A., 2019).

2.4 Green Supply Chain Management (GSCM) - Strategic Perspective

The approach that involves adhering to environmental standards during a product's entire life cycle and design has resulted in the creation of green supply chains (Srivastava, S.K., 2007). Managing these supply chains with green supply chain management (GSCM) techniques is a widely recognized approach to addressing environmental concerns (R. Abdullah, M. Hassan, and N. Johari, 2014). The unpredictable demand and certification requirements for environmentally friendly products make them challenging to produce, which is why a mixed strategy with continuous environmental performance improvement is often emphasized (Zhu & Sarkis, 2004). GSCM can benefit businesses with significant energy consumption by reducing environmental costs, increasing environmental benefits, and alleviating environmental and social responsibility concerns (Bochao Liu, 2023). Environmental considerations are incorporated into the green supply chain throughout the various stages of a product's life cycle, including conception, manufacturing, usage, recycling, reuse, and re-introduction. The green supply chain's performance is evaluated using the "Triple Bottom Line," which considers the impacts on the economy, society, and the environment (Sarkis et al., 2011; Pullman et al., 2009). Many studies have investigated management practices in operational and strategic contexts using the framework of ecological sustainability (Acquaye, Adolf, Genovese, Andrea, Barrett, John, Lenny Koh, S.C., 2014). Other studies have examined the greening of supply chains in different contexts, such as product design (Yu, Wantao, Chavez, Roberto, Feng, Mengying, Wiengarten, Frank, 2013; Alexander, Anthony, Walker, Helen, Aim, Mohamed, 2014). Consequently, large companies are developing innovative approaches to managing multi-tier supply chains to minimize these chain liabilities (Hartmann and Moeller, 2014). GSCM is focused on enhancing market competitiveness and promoting green products (Kumar et al., 2012). Effective management and planning of logistics operations in supply chains require a partner-oriented approach since the delivery process has become an essential aspect of a manufacturer's product offering (Whipple and Frankel, 2006). For companies, maintaining relationships within the supply chain is still a crucial task with competitive ramifications. In the current era, characterized by specialization and global rivalry, businesses rely heavily on supply chain partners to meet customer expectations and differentiate themselves from competitors. For example, Apple depended on Samsung to produce high-resolution retina displays that were a key feature of its iPhones and computers (Smith, 2012). Corporate supply chain sustainability has become a competitive advantage topic in the rapidly changing global environment in recent years. The term "sustainability" has also been incorporated into the majority of community structures, and local organizations, governments, academic institutions, businesses, cooperatives, and supply networks for large corporations have all proposed addressing the issue (Korosh Emamisaleh, Kamaleddin Rahmani, Soleyman Iranzadeh, 2018).

The awareness of the negative impact of industrial practices on the environment has led to the global spread of the "green movement" in supply chains. As a result, companies face increased costs associated with energy consumption and a negative reputation among customers for their lack of environmental awareness. To achieve a balance in economic, social, and environmental performance, players in the supply chain need to innovate and reform in areas such as products, processes, markets, technologies, resource allocation, and organization (Shan et al., 2020).

In the United States, food loss costs an estimated $166 billion per year, with most wasted food ending up in landfills. While experts disagree on the actual amount of food lost, it is clear that inefficient practices during production, processing, transportation, storage, and consumption have negative impacts on the economy and the environment. Therefore, quantifying food loss at each stage of the supply chain, while considering dietary patterns, is crucial (Kim et al., 2020).

China faces a significant challenge in solid waste management due to the large amount of garbage generated, but it has made progress in converting waste to energy. China is now the fourth-largest consumer of waste-to-energy (WTE), with increased capacity from 2 million to 14 million tonnes and over 100 WTE plants. Through this initiative, China produces electricity for $30 per MWH (Gisela Aguilar Dorantes et al., 2019). Meanwhile, Abu Dhabi's Masdar City, built with an investment of $22 billion, operates entirely on renewable energy and is home to over 1500 firms contributing to eco-friendly technologies through research and development efforts. Masdar City also has a solar-powered desalination facility for its water supply and a no-car policy (Shi et al., 2020).

Saudi Arabia, with its abundant sunlight and vast open spaces, is poised to become the top global solar energy exporter, surpassing China (Parajuli et al., 2020).

Even though numerous additional organizational theories exist, we identify a few that show some promise for helping to further understand and explain GSCM. Further investigation of these theories is necessary due to the paucity of GSCM-based research that has sought to investigate their applicability. The four organizational theories we introduce here include (1) Diffusion of Innovation; (2) Path Dependency; (3) Social Embeddedness; and (4) Structuration theories. We provide just a brief description of potential research questions that may be investigated in GSCM with each of these theories.

Diffusion of innovation theory

Diffusion of innovation suggests that innovation is communicated through particular channels, over time, among the members of a social system (Rogers, 2003). Innovations arise to address organizational or technological challenges and the adoption of innovations is most likely for those firms encountering pressures to address those challenges (Kraatz and Zajac, 1996). One important note is that even where adoption of the innovation yields limited results among early adopters, rapid increases may still be observed among other firms facing similar pressures. In the GSCM implementation, these pressures can arise from customer requests, regulatory requirements, and the need for performance improvement on an eco-efficiency (Zhu et al., 2007). This theory also suggests that the diffusion of GSCM as an innovation can be viewed as a process of initiation, persuasion, planning, adoption, and confirmation. Researchers can extend this theory by studying the diffusion of GSCM in different stages and if the proactive, early adopters can garner larger performance gains as posited by aspects of this theory.

Path dependency theory

The focus of path dependency is based on the idea that the initial choices made by decision-makers result in an increasing return (Pierson, 2000). As there are larger rather than smaller benefits to reinforce activity, other choices are prohibitive and thus restrict the decision makers' future choice options to the choice previously made (David, 1985). Even though original applications were for technology, social programs may also be explained by path dependency. Even though at the organizational level, path dependency has been well articulated for organizational change, the expansion to inter-organizational change has also occurred. For example, previous experiences with partner firms are more likely to lead to strategic alliances by these firms (Gulati and Gargiulo, 1999; Chou et al., 2010). Firms implementing a management initiative, e.g., GSCM, in a particular way will yield an effect leading them to do something next time in a similar manner. The implication is that once partner firms in the supply chain have chosen to adopt GSCM, they become "locked in" to its implementation due to many potential reasons such as the initial large set-up costs involved, learning effects, coordination effects, or adaptive expectation that result from its implementation. Path dependency would argue that implementing GSCM can be self-reinforcing and improve as there are more adopters to gain experience that guides further development. This link is a positive-feedback loop: the more people that adopt a technology or a management approach such as GSCM, the more it improves and the more attractive it is for further adoption. Following the insights by North (1990) with his introduction of the institutional matrix, further research can extend this path dependency perspective by examining the implementation of GSCM as a self-reinforcing mechanism contingent on initial conditions, supply chain relationships, a commitment of partner firms, and the sequence of implementing different GSCM dimension.

Social embeddedness theory

Firms are embedded in ongoing networks of social relationships (Granovetter, 1985). This social embeddedness perspective enables us to understand the embeddedness of partner firms in a supply chain on implementing GSCM. Embeddedness is a process of becoming part of a structure such as GSCM. Such embeddedness can be characterized by the strength of the social ties of a firm with its immediate social context, which is useful for enterprises to identify social resources. In the embedding process, firms need to understand the nature of the structure, e.g., the different dimensions of GSCM. Then, they will enact and reenact this structure which forges new ties and subsequently maintains both the link and the structure. A highly embedded supply chain allows access to support for environmental management initiatives and increases partner cooperation in pursuit of GSCM. Alternatively, the embeddedness can also be a liability constraining organizational actions (Uzzi, 1997). For instance, the unforeseeable exit of a core partner, e.g., a major supplier, can disrupt the efforts on the eco-design of products to serve the supply chain. The relationships of social embeddedness to the social network theory may also be investigated.

Structuration theory

Structuration theory (Giddens, 1984) can be a useful framework to better understand the nexus of implementing GSCM and the driving forces as it theorizes the interdependence of the actor (agent) and the context (structure). Structuration theory specifies a reciprocal relationship between agency and structure with a view on duality, where they co-evolve to shape environmental management approaches such as GSCM to strive for environmental and productivity gains. This structuration view is useful for explaining complex social interactions, and specifically in GSCM, the interaction of the different actors (agents) including customers and suppliers in the GSCM implementation (structure) should be understood collectively. Within a structuration framework, the involved actors are conceptualized as agents acting with social and economic systems that engender potentially rewarding opportunities through GSCM. Insights can be obtained on how these actors apply rules, knowledge, and resources in interaction, and as such guide the actions of enterprises on GSCM implementation in adapting to their requirements.

Agency theory

Agency theory focuses on scenarios that one entity, the principal, authorizes a second, the agent, to act on the principal's behalf (Eisenhardt, 1989). The theory focuses on the costs arising from conflicts of interest between managers and stockholders (for example, over the amount of effort to be exerted, risk being borne, shirking, and perquisites tradeoffs between the pursuit of sales versus profits). Part of this tension arises when environmental and financial goals within organizations may potentially conflict. There are situations where agents often behave in ways that benefit them, not principals. For example, a CEO may exploit his/her role as an agent by adopting a particular management practice to improve their compensation, regardless of the actual benefit of the management practice to the company. It has also been argued that Agency theory offers a natural fit with supply chain management research (Ketchen and Hult, 2007).

Some research has investigated agency theory as a lens to explain the adoption of general environmental management practices (Cordeiro and Sarkis, 2008; Berrone and Go´mez-Mejia, 2009). The issue of compensation, incentives, and general motivation of upper-level management has been a major focus of agency theory applications to corporate environmental management. In one of the few studies in this area pertinent to GSCM, Kogg (2003) argues that greening the supply chain can be achieved through the use of power leverage and incentives. Thorough investigations of the role of agency theory in motivating managers in dyadic or supply chain situations (for example, as a benefit to the relationship versus a benefit to specific organizational stockholders) are clear areas for research. Specifically, future research on this topic could investigate how individual-level (e.g., CEO and senior executives) and firm-level (e.g., contractors and suppliers) reward structures promote the adoption of GSCM. Whether multi-level, and cross-organizational, congruencies exist in compensation and reward systems and the impact on the adoption of GSCM practices, and their performance are additional questions that can be evaluated.

2.5 Green Supply Chain Management - Eco-Friendly Practices in India

"Green supply chain management (GSCM) is defined as the practice of improving environmental performance along with the supply chain, including product design, customer relations, and operations management (Srivastava, 2007)." Green supply-chain management (GrSCM) involves incorporating environmental considerations into various aspects of supply-chain management, including product design, material sourcing and selection, manufacturing processes, product delivery to consumers, and end-of-life management (Agyabeng-Mensah et al., 2020). The concept of GrSCM is derived from the literature on supply-chain management and environmental management, which emphasizes the importance of addressing the effects and relationships between supply-chain management and the environment. The boundaries of GrSCM are determined by the investigator's aims, and the literature on GrSCM includes topics such as green purchasing, integrated green supply chains, and reverse logistics (Geng et al., 2020).

GrSCM has applications in waste management, resource conservation, and environmental risk management (Petljak et al., 2018). It encompasses activities related to the production, handling, usage, transportation, and disposal of products, intending to minimize the ecological footprint by employing sustainable materials and methods (Setyaning et al., 2020). Waste minimization involves decreasing the amount of hazardous waste produced during operations and production (Maruglio, 2014).

Reverse logistics refers to managing the flow of raw materials, finished products, and associated information from the point of consumption back to the point of origin efficiently and cost-effectively, with the primary objective of recovering value or ensuring appropriate disposal of the materials involved (Sayed et al., 2017). In other words, reverse logistics can be defined as, "The process of planning, implementing, and controlling the efficient, cost-effective flow of raw materials, in- process inventory, finished goods, and related information from the point of consumption to the point of origin for recapturing value or proper disposal (Rogers and Tibben-Lembke, 1999)."

Several multinational corporations, such as Nestle and Heineken, have implemented eco-friendly measures to address environmental concerns. Nestle has implemented water disposal systems and aims to achieve "zero waste for disposal," while Heineken has a program called "Aware of Energy" that focuses on educating workers about energy-related issues and aims to reduce its carbon footprint (Geng et al., 2020).

The following information highlights the efforts made by Indian businesses to adopt eco-friendly practices in their supply chain management, with a focus on sustainability. The sources cited in this information are given below:

1. ITC - ITC is a multinational corporation that operates in various sectors and is well-known for promoting eco-friendly practices. The information mentioned the company's green measures, such as ECF technology, ozone bleaching, water and energy management strategies, and environmentally friendly boiler systems, which help the company cut down its reliance on non-renewable energy sources like coal. The information also stated that ITC recycles waste products to manufacture paperboard for packaging and has implemented e-choupals, which provide the company with a competitive edge in sustainable raw materials and generated profits.
2. Dr. Reddy's - The pharma industry in India is under pressure to reduce its environmental impact, and Dr. Reddy's is one company that places a high priority on sustainable sourcing. The information mentioned the company's mentoring program, which provides regular,

high-quality training to its vendors, especially new business partners, on how to implement sustainable business practices.

3. L&T - Larsen & Toubro Limited (L&T) is an engineering and construction company that utilizes the 3R principle (reduce, recycle, and reuse) in many of its initiatives. The information mentioned that the company gathers more than 23 million gallons of rainwater, has reduced water usage by 6%, and has had 16 campuses without any wastewater discharge. L&T also heavily relies on renewable energy sources like wind and solar electricity throughout its facilities and uses recycled materials for its raw material requirements, such as fly ash and crushed sand.
4. TCS - Tata Consultancy Services (TCS) has increased the usage of renewable energy in its workplaces and places a strong emphasis on using green suppliers. The information mentioned TCS's internal programs and discussions with staff members about the benefits of energy conservation and utilizing sewage treatment facilities, rainwater collection systems, and other water management techniques to reduce the consumption of freshwater by about 13%. TCS also encourages the use of video conferencing in all its sites to reduce employee travel to client locations by automobile and cut greenhouse gas emissions.
5. State Bank of India - SBI Bank has launched a ground-breaking initiative called the "Green Channel Counter" to enable paperless banking. The information mentioned that an account holder can transfer, withdraw, and deposit money into another account without any physical paperwork, and the bank has also installed solar-powered ATMs in rural areas to utilize 1000 watts less energy than conventional ATMs.
6. Oil and Natural Gas Company (ONGC) - ONGC has developed an eco-friendly, energy-efficient cremation method in collaboration with the Mokshda Paryavaran Evam Van Suraksha Samiti. The information mentioned that the innovation will contribute to a 60% reduction in wood use and a significant reduction in air and water pollution.

2.6 Green Supply Chain Variables

2.6.1 Reverse Logistics (RL)

"Green distribution refers to the integration of environmental considerations into distribution and logistics operations, intending to reduce the environmental impact of these processes. Green logistics covers reverse logistics and green distribution. The term "Reverse Logistics" (RL) refers to managing the flow of raw materials, in-process inventory, finished products, and related data from the point of consumption back to the point of origin to recapture value or ensure proper disposal (Govindan, Jepsen, & Schauder, 2019; Rogers and Tibben-Lembke, 1999). Reverse logistics differ from regular logistics (Carter and Ellram, 1998) and involves coordination between two or more markets, managing supply unpredictability, making decisions on returns disposition, implementing postponement strategies, and engaging in speculation (Yalabik et al., 2005), affecting network architecture.

The collection is the first phase of recovery, where items are located, gathered, and transported to locations for remanufacturing (Krikke et al., 1998). Inspection and sorting require skill in classifying used items (Ferrer and Whybark, 2000), and environmentally friendly logistics techniques are necessary (Wu and Dunn, 1995). Reverse logistics programs have significant benefits and require methodologies for development and implementation (Poist, 2000; Stock et al., 2002; Tibben-Lembke, 2002). The optimal arrangement of infrastructure and transportation networks is necessary for transferring pre-owned goods from previous owners to manufacturers and forthcoming markets (Fleischmann et al., 2001).

Businesses need to focus on RL tactics, which may impact their bottom line (Srivastava and Srivastava, 2005). Developing a hierarchical decision-making framework to evaluate profit-driven RL networks is essential. Companies view RL acts as profitable for their specific product category, and integrating GSCM operations would depend heavily on information and communication technology (ICT) (Dekker et al., 2004). RL operations can be integrated within an organization (Chouinard et al., 2005), and investing in information technology improves RL performance (Daugherty et al., 2005).

The use of quantitative techniques like mixed integer linear programming (MILP) models is common in "forward logistics" systems (Mirchandani and Francis, 1989). However, a standard set of models for reverse logistics networks is yet to be established. Fleischmann et al. (2000) reviewed nine case studies on recovery networks in different industries, including recycling carpet (Louwers et al., 1999), recycling steel production by-products (Barros et al., 1998), recycling electronics (Jayaraman et al., 1999; Krikke et al., 1998), recycling reusable containers (Kroon and Vrijens, 1995), and recycling sand from demolition waste (Louwers et al., 1999), and examined the resulting network architecture in various contexts. Recently, numerous studies on quantitative reverse logistics approaches have been published (Shih, 2001). One such study discusses Taiwan's reverse logistics system for recycling computers and gadgets in detail. Hu et al. (2002) published a cost-minimization model for a multi-time-step, multi-type hazardous-waste reverse logistics system. Nagurney and Toyasaki's approach to modeling the electronic waste reverse logistics network includes recycling, while Srivastava and Srivastava's (2007) paradigm includes three different types of rework facilities. Ravi et al. (2005) used the analytical network process (ANP) and a balanced scorecard to analyze reverse logistics choices for end-of-life computers. Listes and Dekker (2005) offer a stochastic programming-based method for extending a deterministic location model to explicitly take uncertainties into account for creating a product recovery network. They apply it in a case study on the Dutch recycling of sand from construction waste and offer useful advice on how to make judgments in an uncertain reverse logistics environment based on their analysis of the data. Mostard and Teunter (2006) did a case study to generate a simple closed-form equation to determine the ideal order quantity based on the demand distribution, the likelihood that a sold item would be returned, and all relevant revenues and outlays for a single period model. Min et al. (2006) solved the reverse logistics problem involving product returns using a non-linear mixed-integer programming model and a genetic algorithm to determine the number and location of centralized return centers. Reverse logistics is a crucial component of green logistics and a crucial component of GSCM that allows organizations to use logistics in a way that yields both economic and environmental benefits by conserving previously utilized resources (Zhu et al., 2008; Gandhi et al., 2015).

2.6.2 Green Inclination

Verfuerth et al. (2018) defined green inclination as an organization's motivation to adopt environmentally sustainable practices and reduce its environmental impact. Similarly, Luchs et al. (2010) defined green inclination as a consumer's willingness to pay more for environmentally friendly products. Gifford and Nilsson (2014) found that social influence can be a significant motivator for green inclination, as individuals who perceive their peers engaging in environmentally friendly behaviors are more likely to adopt those behaviors themselves. Due to the increased business climate instability and unpredictability, interest in supply chain resilience (SCR) has grown among scholars and practitioners (Al-Hakimi and Borade, 2020; Parast and Shekarian, 2019).

"In other words, Green Inclination is the extent to which an organization is motivated to adopt environmentally sustainable practices and reduce its environmental impact. The green inclination is a combination of customer orientation and Organizational Involvement. Higher orientation toward green supply chain practices by an organization leads to greater customer orientation and better corporate growth (Verfuerth et al., 2018)." De Groot and Steg (2018) found that environmental education can promote green inclination by increasing individuals' sense of personal responsibility for the environment. Similarly, Kim and Lee (2018) found that personal values play an important role in shaping green inclination, as individuals who place a higher value on environmental concerns are more likely to engage in pro-environmental behaviors due to their sense of moral obligation to protect the environment.

Various studies have examined the drivers of green inclination. Environmental concern, knowledge, and perceived behavioral control were the most powerful predictors of green inclination among individuals (Bamberg & Möser, 2007), while young adults' values, norms, and attitudes toward sustainability were significant predictors (Steg et al., 2014). Organizational culture and leadership also influenced firms' green inclination (Delmas & Toffel, 2008), and Arora and Cason (1996) found that environmental regulations affected firms' adoption of eco-friendly technologies. Social norms and identity were linked to green inclination in studies by Thøgersen (2006) and Gatersleben et al. (2002). Nonetheless, environmental concern did not always correspond to eco-friendly behaviors, as Vermeir and Verbeke (2006) discovered.

2.6.3 Green Techno Marketing

In recent years, there has been a surge in the development of green technology, and marketing of such products has become an essential element in achieving sustainable economic growth. The green technology market can be challenging due to its complexity and dynamism (Zhang & Liu, 2021). To meet the demand for eco-friendly products, companies are producing green technologies and goods.

To attract environmentally conscious customers, companies must emphasize the environmental benefits of their products in their marketing strategies (Rana et al., 2021). Additionally, companies must focus on promoting a superior performance by aligning green technology and green marketing that makes green techno marketing (Yoo & Gretzel, 2021). Collaborating with merchants and distributors who specialize in ecologically friendly goods can help companies efficiently reach their target consumers (Hultman & Luchs, 2021). By developing a better understanding of consumers' reasons for choosing green products, companies can market their green products to increase sales and encourage consumers to switch from non-green products (Acharya & Gupta, 2016).

One of the current trends in Indian business is green marketing, which involves meeting the needs of society and customers in a way that is helpful and long-lasting, to reduce the harmful environmental effects of consumption and production (Pujari & Wright, 1996; Polonsky, 2005). Although studies on customer purchasing habits for environmentally friendly items exist, green marketing involves all marketing initiatives created to support customers' environmental attitudes and behaviors (Mostafa, 2007). By implementing green innovation, businesses can boost productivity and enhance environmental management performance to fulfill the requirements of environmental protection (Chen, 2008; Lai et al., 2003).

Green marketing can contribute significantly to the social normalization of green practices and products by presenting them as commonplace and routine rather than emphasizing their "green" nature (Rettie et al., 2014). Several studies have emphasized the significance of green techno-marketing in promoting environmentally sustainable practices and products. Consumers are willing to pay a premium for products marketed as environmentally friendly, especially if they perceive them to be of higher quality (Hartmann et al., 2005). Furthermore, green techno-marketing can enhance a company's reputation and increase customer loyalty (Chan et al., 2011).

2.6.4 Green Purchase

The concept of "green purchase" or "environmentally friendly purchase" refers to a consumer's decision to buy goods or services that are less harmful to the environment compared to other options. According to Dorjgotov et al. (2021), green purchasing involves considering environmental aspects such as the production process, packaging, disposal, and overall environmental impact of the product. The goal of green purchasing is to work with suppliers to provide environmentally friendly items (Zhu et al., 2008), and it involves making strategic purchasing decisions based on eco-friendly criteria, including waste reduction and the potential for product reuse and recycling (De Sousa Jabbour et al., 2015).

Consumers' motivation for making green purchases can be intrinsic, stemming from their values, beliefs, and desire to act responsibly in society, or extrinsic, influenced by marketing messages or incentives (Sharma et al., 2021). Green purchasing management involves implementing environmentally conscious purchasing practices that promote recycling and reclamation while still meeting performance requirements and reducing waste (CHUN et al., 2015). Research shows that adopting such practices can positively impact a company's operational performance, particularly when long-term supplier relationships are established (Cassia Regina Bianchini et al., 2018).

To make an ecological purchase, source reduction through recycling, reusing, altering, and controlling materials is essential, and supplier development is critical (Burritt et al., 2011; Pazirandeh and Jafari, 2013). Green purchasing is vital for businesses to improve their environmental friendliness and operational efficiency (Lo and Shiah, 2016). Numerous studies have highlighted the importance of green purchasing in reducing environmental impacts, improving a company's reputation and competitiveness, and even leading to cost savings over time (Pagiaslis and Krontalis, 2014; Mohan et al., 2017).

2.6.5 Green Products

"Environmental orientation refers to the degree to which individuals or organizations prioritize and act upon environmental concerns in their decision-making and behaviors". Environmental orientation focuses on Green product that requires a core focus on Green Manufacturing and Green design (Jansson, Marell, & Nordlund, 2011). Green products are goods that have a reduced impact on the environment, as they are created, produced, and distributed sustainably or using recycled materials (Biege et al., 2021) while green design is a core focus on designing sustainable processes for sustainable development. Sustainable development, which seeks to balance economic, social, and environmental factors, is closely linked to green products in the world of product design and production (Kumar et al., 2021). Studies have identified several key characteristics of green products that matter to consumers, such as perceived environmental benefits, product quality, and cost, as well as certifications, brand reputation, and availability of environmental impact information (Dangelico & Pujari, 2021). Life Cycle Assessment (LCA) is an evaluation tool used to assess a product's environmental impact throughout its life cycle, from raw material extraction to disposal, helping companies identify areas for improvement (Goglio et al., 2021). Energy and life-cycle approaches have been developed for analyzing flow systems to minimize resource use and energy consumption (Al-Shboul & Moh'd Anwer, 2017).

Green products also include recycling, which recovers raw materials from old and broken products and is driven by governmental and economic factors, with logistics accounting for up to 95% of total expenditures in the recycling industry (Calì et al., 2022). The automobile and consumer electronics industries use economically motivated recycling (de Fazio et al., 1997; Johnson, 1998). Green products are a combination of recycling, reuse, and remanufacturing, with Melissen and de Ron (1999) providing recovery protocols and relevant terminology. According to Krikke et al. (1998), common examples of green products are paper, electronics, and automobiles (Nasr, 2011; Shrivastava, 1995; Tan et al., 2002). Recycling is also considered a crucial aspect of green products, which involves breaking down a product into its constituent parts (Taleb and Gupta, 1997). Reusing products and resources is another important aspect of green products (Thierry et al., 1995).

Green products are goods that are produced, distributed, and consumed with consideration for the environment to reduce their negative impact (Amin & Khan, 2021). They help mitigate environmental issues such as climate change, deforestation, air and water pollution, and biodiversity loss associated with the production and consumption of goods and services (Hsu & Li, 2016). Green products also provide economic benefits such as job creation and reduced healthcare costs from pollution-related illnesses (Fellner, 2019). Adopting green products promotes a circular economy and reduces greenhouse gas emissions while conserving natural resources (Liu & Li, 2021).

2.6.6 Environmental Orientation

Environmental orientation refers to the degree to which individuals or organizations prioritize and act on environmental issues in their decision-making and behaviors (Jansson, Marell, & Nordlund, 2011). Studies have shown that individuals with a strong environmental orientation are more likely to engage in eco-friendly behaviors, such as recycling, taking public transportation, and reducing energy consumption (Schahn & Holzer, 1990; Stern et al., 1999). Similarly, businesses that prioritize the environment are more likely to adopt sustainable practices, reduce their carbon footprint, and comply with environmental regulations (Epstein & Roy, 2001; Russo & Fouts, 1997). However, it is important to note that individuals with strong environmental orientations may engage in "greenwashing," which refers to environmentally symbolic behaviors that have little practical impact on the environment (Hobson, Burke, & Pearse, 2006). Reverse logistics practices can be implemented by manufacturers to reduce pollution by reducing the burden of end-of-life products on the environment (Muhammad Waqas et al., 2018).

2.6.7 Green Distribution

The concept of green distribution involves incorporating environmental considerations into distribution and logistics practices to reduce any negative environmental impacts (Govindan, Jepsen, & Schauder, 2019). Numerous strategies can be implemented to enhance the eco-friendliness of distribution operations, such as using electric or hybrid vehicles to decrease emissions and boost fuel efficiency (Kleyner & Stavins, 2018). Other approaches include optimizing delivery routes and utilizing real-time data to minimize empty miles, thereby reducing fuel consumption and emissions (Govindan et al., 2019). The use of environmentally friendly packaging materials, such as recycled paper or biodegradable plastics, can also help to minimize waste (Kumar, Scheibe, & Weber, 2020). Nonetheless, there are challenges associated with implementing green distribution strategies, such as the substantial up-front expenses involved in deploying sustainable technologies and the difficulty of managing complex distribution networks (Govindan et al., 2019).

To stay innovative, attractive, competitive, and successful in today's ever-changing and unique marketing environment, companies need to focus on the commendable approach of green distribution (Ahmed, Syed Shakil; Akter, Tauhima; Ma, Yuchao, 2018). The objective of green distribution is to minimize the negative impact of transportation on the environment. According to research, various studies have been conducted to develop more efficient distribution networks and optimize transportation routes to reduce fuel consumption and greenhouse gas emissions (Li et al., 2021). The significance of green distribution is critical in reducing the negative impact of transportation on the environment. The transportation sector is responsible for roughly 23% of global greenhouse gas emissions, making it a significant contributor to climate change (UNEP, 2017). The adoption of green distribution practices not only helps to reduce carbon emissions but also improves air quality and promotes sustainable development (Zhang et al., 2021). Additionally, green distribution has economic benefits, including lower transportation costs, increased efficiency, and improved brand reputation (Jain & Singh, 2019).

2.6.8 Normative Pressure

Normative pressures are a key factor in shaping both internal and external practices of Green Supply Chain Management (GSCM) (Vanalle et al., 2017). The activation perspective of normative pressure suggests that ethical standards can be translated into environmentally responsible behavior, which promotes green social norms through green purchasing behavior. Consumers' growing desire to protect the environment and purchase sustainable and environmentally friendly products also drives this trend (Hazaea et al., 2022; Kalpande & Toke, 2021).

Studies have shown that normative and coercive pressures positively impact the adoption of eco-friendly practices in GSCM, resulting in higher environmental performance for organizations (Zhu et al., 2013). In particular, pressures from suppliers, customers, and the market are crucial for Chinese manufacturers in adopting internal practices related to environmental management (IEM) and eco-friendliness (ECO). A study by Toke (2021) explores how Indian manufacturers can achieve sustainable development through the implementation of green supply chain management practices and examines the performance, pressures, and barriers associated with such practices. In developing nations, normative pressures mainly come from strategic buyers and suppliers from wealthy nations, who are the primary motivators for adopting green practices (Chandra Shukla et al., 2009). The term "normative pressure" refers to how social norms, values, and expectations can impact a person's attitudes and behaviors (Cialdini & Goldstein, 2004). Research has shown that normative pressure significantly influences people's attitudes and behaviors. For instance, people may follow group norms to win social acceptance or to avoid social rejection (Asch, 1951). Institutional pressure, including normative, coercive, and mimetic forces, has the potential to affect how responsive a company is to GSCM project acceptance (Kalpande, 2021).

2.6.9 Institutional Pressure

Institutional pressure refers to the influence of external institutions, such as industry norms and laws, on the adoption of sustainable supply chain practices (Diabat, Govindan, & Kannan, 2017) Institutional pressure has been found to have a significant impact on the adoption of green supply chain practices. For example, government incentives and restrictions can encourage businesses to invest in eco-friendly technologies (Chen, Geng, Fujita, & Zhu, 2014). The sources of institutional pressure that compel businesses to adopt green practices are social, market, and regulatory. Regulatory pressure stems from government regulations and norms, while market pressure originates from customers and suppliers who demand environmentally friendly practices. NGOs and other sustainability advocates exert social pressure (Klassen and Vereecke, 2012). Institutional forces significantly influence organizations' adoption of internal GSCM practices. For example, the European Union has implemented environmental laws, such as the Restriction of Hazardous Substances (RoHS), Waste Electrical and Electronic Equipment (WEEE), End of Life Vehicles (ELV), and others, to ensure that industrial activities have a minimal negative environmental impact (Yu, W.; Ramanathan, R., 2015). The role of institutional processes in shaping supplier behavior has also been studied. Seuring and Muller (2008) examined the impact of institutional pressures on supplier compliance with environmental standards. They found that regulatory and market pressures were important drivers of supplier compliance, but that the effectiveness of these pressures depended on factors such as supplier size and industry sector.

2.6.10 Organizational Involvement

According to Kleindorfer, Singhal, and Wassenhove (2005), the extent to which a company actively promotes environmental sustainability through its supply chain practices is known as organizational participation. Studies have shown that companies that prioritize sustainability are more likely to invest in eco-friendly products and methods and work with suppliers to improve their environmental performance (Mol, 2007). Additionally, businesses with a strong environmental focus are more likely to view sustainability as a competitive advantage and prioritize sustainable supply chain practices (Pagell & Shevchenko, 2014). Several factors can influence the degree of organizational involvement in green supply chain management, including the perceived importance of sustainability to the company, access to resources and knowledge, and support from senior management (Kleindorfer et al., 2005; Mol, 2007). Furthermore, external factors such as government legislation and consumer demand for sustainable goods and services can also impact an organization's involvement (Pagell & Shevchenko, 2014).

According to Joseph Sarkis, Kee-hung Lai, and Yong Geng (2008), Green supply chain management (GSCM) has become a critical competitive strategy for businesses involved in global trade due to economic globalization, resource scarcity, and environmental degradation. The literature on organizational involvement in the supply chain emphasizes the importance of improving communication and collaboration among supply chain partners. To achieve an effective supply chain, many studies have highlighted the importance of building strong relationships with suppliers and customers (Fawcett et al., 2018).

Utilizing technology to improve collaboration and coordination is crucial in supply chain engagement. Many businesses are implementing digital platforms and technologies to enhance supply chain visibility, coordination, and communication (Zheng et al., 2019). The role of organizational culture in promoting cooperation and participation in the supply chain is another essential area of research. A company's culture can shape employee attitudes toward teamwork and their willingness to participate in collaborative activities. Companies that value collaboration are more likely to develop supply chain alliances and perform better overall, according to studies (Bello et al., 2017).

2.6.11 Customer Cooperation

Incorporating incentives to promote sustainable behavior is a vital aspect of customer collaboration in green supply chains. Eco-labeling, green pricing, and loyalty programs are some tactics that businesses are using to encourage customers to support sustainable practices (Rahman et al., 2017). Educating customers about the impact of their consumption choices on the environment and the benefits of adopting sustainable practices is crucial for promoting customer engagement in green supply chain practices (Umar Burki, 2019). Social norms have a significant influence on customers' attitudes toward sustainable practices, and businesses can leverage this effect to encourage customers to embrace sustainable practices (Vining and Ebreo, 2015). Businesses must recognize customers as strategic partners to address environmental challenges, with their involvement spanning from eco-design through distribution, including product returns and packaging. Customer cooperation throughout the supply chain is essential, and building long-term relationships based on trust is crucial for the effective sharing of real-time information and the smooth execution of all green supply chain processes (Bouzon et al., 2018; Eltayeb et al., 2011).

2.6.12 Green Manufacturing

In recent years, there have been several studies on green manufacturing and its importance in achieving sustainable production. Cheng et al. (2022) emphasized the significance of green manufacturing in addressing environmental challenges and promoting sustainable development. Wong et al. (2022) identified the need for more research on green manufacturing practices, stakeholder engagement, regulatory frameworks, and technological innovation. Jafarian et al. (2021) highlighted the key themes in the literature on green manufacturing, as well as the challenges and barriers to its adoption. Yalcin and Aras (2021) discussed the economic, environmental, and social benefits of green manufacturing, as well as the need for collaboration among stakeholders. Singh et al. (2021) conducted a systematic review of green manufacturing practices and their impact on the environment. Together, these studies emphasize the importance of green manufacturing in achieving sustainable production and promoting corporate social responsibility, while also identifying the need for more research in this area.

2.6.13 Financial Performance

Several studies have examined the relationship between green supply chain management (GSCM) and financial performance, with mixed results. While some studies have found a positive correlation between the two, suggesting that GSCM practices can enhance financial performance, other research has found a weak or no relationship. Variables such as stakeholder demand, resource availability, and top management support can impact the success of GSCM projects. A study by Mengying Feng et al. (2018) explored the correlation between financial success and GSCM, with operational and environmental performance acting as mediators. They found that implementing a comprehensive sustainable supply chain management approach can have a positive impact on a company's financial performance, but the benefits may not be immediate. Supply chain finance (SCF) has also emerged as a strategy for enhancing the financial performance of supply chains, with research focusing on how SCF solutions can support SC sustainability performance (Tianyu Zhang, 2020). Yubing Yu (2020) found that supplier and customer green management practices can positively impact financial performance, while Masood Nawaz Kalyar et al. (2019) identified GSCM practices such as green manufacturing and eco-design as having a direct impact on financial success.

2.6.14 Social Performance

According to several studies, the implementation of sustainable practices in the supply chain can enhance social performance by improving working conditions, promoting ethical labor practices, and supporting local communities while also advancing environmental sustainability (Carter & Rogers, 2008; Pishvaee, Jolai, & Razmi, 2012; Sarkis et al., 2011). However, the interaction between social performance and GSCM is complex and dependent on various contextual factors, such as the level of stakeholder pressure, availability of resources and skills, level of senior management support, and industry and market setting (Carter & Rogers, 2008; Pishvaee et al., 2012; Sarkis et al., 2011). Green internal integration is connected to both environmental and social performance, providing the foundation for green supplier integration (GSI) and green customer integration (GCI) (Zhaojun Han, Baofeng Huo, 2020; Jing Wang, Jun Dai, 2018). Additionally, a methodology has been proposed to examine how green practices influence the sustainability performance of the supply chain (NADINE KAFA, 2013).

2.6.15 Environmental Performance

Manufacturing companies are increasingly adopting green supply chain management (GSCM) practices to reduce their carbon emissions, minimize water usage, and reduce solid waste (Chandra Shukla et al., 2009). The impact of GSCM on the environment, economy, and operational efficiency has made it a widely debated topic (Eltayeb et al., 2011). Initiatives such as eco-design, sustainable sourcing, recycling, and remanufacturing are being used by businesses to prioritize environmental protection (Anwar Al-Sheyadi and Luc Muyldermans, 2019). A positive correlation between green suppliers, green innovations, and environmental performance has been noted, but there is also a negative correlation between these factors and operational efficiency (Ehsan Khaksar, 2015). Integrating supplier and customer quality can enhance environmental performance (Min Zhang and Yubing Yu, 2017). Organizations are addressing environmental concerns by adopting the notion of an environmentally responsible supply chain (Kittisak Jermsittiparsert, Parinya Siriattakul, and Nuanluk Sangperm, 2019), and studies have shown a positive correlation between GSCM practices and environmental performance (Juuso Toyli, Lauri Ojala, and Sini Laari, 2018).

2.6.16 Operational Performance

The positive relationship between green supply chain management (GSCM) and operational performance has been observed in many studies (Wantao Yu et al., 2014; S. Lee et al., 2013; Ayman Bahjat Abdallah and Wafaa Shihadeh Al-Ghwayeen, 2019). Additionally, the adoption of GSCM practices and ERP systems has been shown to enhance operational performance, particularly in quality, cost-effectiveness, flexibility, and delivery timeliness (Ruben Wahyu Santoso and Hotlan Siagian, 2022; Jiawei Xu et al., 2022). Furthermore, a company's commitment to environmental concerns is a crucial factor in determining the success of its GSCM approaches (Jiawei Xu et al., 2022).

2.7 Significance of this Research Study

Based on the reported studies and in-depth literature as well as inputs received from experts from industry and academia, various parameters for exploring the impact of variables are considered that includes Green Logistics, Institutional Pressure, Social Performance, Operational performance, Green Purchase, Environmental Orientation, Normative Pressure, Financial Performance, Environmental Performance, Green Inclination, Green Products, and Green Techno Marketing.

2.8 Need for Research

Following independence, the Indian economy was considered predominantly an agri-based economy. This was followed by the government's liberalized policies and tendency to boost the manufacturing sector, and as a result, many manufacturing facilities were set up to produce various components. A fresh set of difficulties have emerged as a result of the pressures of privatization, globalization, and liberalization. This calls for a strong focus on effective and efficient supply chain management as the focus shifts from "production centric" to "customer-centric" and toward a "concern for green" approach.

Integration of the supply chain's many stakeholders is necessary for effective management. For a productive and efficient supply chain, Bowersox et al. (1999a, b) also emphasized the significance of achieving integration with customers, suppliers, and other external parties as well as within internal operations. The past two decades have seen a rise in interest in green supply chain activities. This is understandable given that resources are scarce, and dwindling, and the environment's deterioration will further accelerate this dwindling. Even though numerous Indian manufacturing companies began adopting green supply chain management practices in the latter part of the 20th century, there has been limited research conducted thus far to establish a model for studying these practices that can be applied by Indian manufacturing enterprises. The following observations and gaps in the existing literature have been identified. The analysis of the literature makes it abundantly evident that supply chain management initially placed a strong emphasis on efficiency, but as time has passed and academics' perspectives have changed, the field is now seriously considering sustainability metrics and their drivers. Although there have been many scholars studying the topic of green supply chains, their major areas of interest tend to range from modeling different elements to examining conceptual domains. Visualizing green concepts on the Indian manufacturing supply chain appears to have a glaring deficiency. While it is abundantly obvious from the literature that many empirical investigations of GSCM techniques have been undertaken in developed nations, there have been relatively few studies conducted in India and even fewer in Gujarat. Numerous studies have explored different GSCM dimensions and viewpoints, but there is not even a single study like this with a horizontally focused approach who have covered all the variables for concrete findings.

2.9 Chapter Summary

In the context of the reviewed literature, there is broad consensus that GSCM practices are essential for enhancing a company's business performance and that creating performance measurement variables is essential. This chapter discusses elements associated with green supply chain practices and performance is to be examined. The proposed research paradigm and the hypotheses will be analyzed in the upcoming chapter

CHAPTER-3

Research Methodology

3.1 Research Problem

Green Supply Chain Performance requires focused study and green practices impart an important place in modern times (Buyukozkan & Cifci, 2012). There have been a few comprehensive studies on green supply chain management carried out particularly in India, providing researchers an opportunity to investigate the concept in further detail for manufacturing enterprises. Kumar, Teichman, and Timpernagel (2012) concluded that GSCM practices lead to cost-saving and efficiency improvement. In line with the same, the researcher has decided to work over the research gap for a comprehensive study to assess the GSCM strategies employed by manufacturing firms and understand the degree of green awareness among manufacturing companies across Gujarat. Organizations have increasingly adopted GSCM practices over time, and this study seeks to understand the impact of adopting GSCM practices on organizational performance.

3.2 Research Gap

As economies increasingly move towards embracing global supply chains, there is a pressing need to pay attention to bringing down the environmental impact of these supply chains. One such emerging alternative concept is that of green supply chain management which amalgamates the effectiveness of supply chains with concern for environmental impact (Nandini Gajendrum,2017). From the literature review, it is evident that Green practices in the Supply chain are followed in Western countries. But in India, particularly in Gujarat, very few comprehensive studies are done on Green supply chain management. This provides the researcher with the opportunity to carry out a comprehensive study on the concept of Green Supply Chain Management in manufacturing companies of Gujarat.

3.3 Research Objectives

As previously noted, analyzing the awareness of GSCM practices in industries is crucial. Over time, there has been an observed increase in the adoption of GSCM by organizations. In this study, the researcher aimed to examine the effect of implementing GSCM practices on organizational performance across manufacturing firms in Gujarat. There are three research objectives as mentioned below:

1. To measure awareness of GSCM practices amongst manufacturing firms of Gujarat.
2. To identify GSCM practices adopted by the selected companies of Gujarat.
3. To investigate the impact of the adoption of GSCM practices on organizational performance

3.4 Research Design

The basis for the execution of research talks about the right conduct of research effectively and efficiently is known as the research design. It is a strategy that seeks to specify when, how, and most importantly where data will be gathered and analyzed (Parahoo, 1997). To put it differently, the concept of research design refers to a structured plan or model for conducting a study to achieve maximum control over variables that may affect the accuracy of the findings (Burns and Grove, 2003). As described by Polit et al. (2001), the research design represents the researcher's overall approach to a specific research question or examination of a hypothesis. The main components of the research design are as follows:-

a) Descriptive research.

3.4.1 Type of Research

a) Descriptive research.

The type of research is descriptive research to assess a specific hypothesis. A definitive descriptive study helps describe the features and represent large representative samples after exploratory research has looked at the concept of the GSCM. Descriptive research is helpful to examine and respond to the particular study hypothesis employing a survey approach. The three main components of a survey method are the gathering of data, quantitative data analysis, and the use of a sample to represent the community. The most preferred strategy, according to Malhotra and Grover, is to generalize the links indicated by the research hypothesis. Here, survey design refers to the procedure of creating a sample plan, creating the questionnaire, and analyzing the data. As a survey method, a survey strategy is used. The survey process makes use of a structured questionnaire. The researcher has designed a formal questionnaire and used it to pose questions in a present order to collect organized data.

3.4.2 Target Population Definition

3.4.1.1 Target Population

The term "target population" refers to a particular group of individuals or things for which particular data are gathered or observations are conducted to create the necessary data structure and information. In other terms, a target population is a group of components or a group of things that a researcher is interested to learn more about and from which inferences must be drawn. The target audience transforms the problem definition into a particular, exact statement. Who should be included in the sample is expressly stated in the target population. **Here, Target Population** is manufacturing firms engaged in green supply chain strategies. The element can be defined as an object that possesses a piece of information that is sought by the researcher. Here, the element is a **manufacturing firm involved in green supply chain practices**

3.4.1.2 Survey Approach

A **personal survey approach** is employed as a survey technique to measure the impact of green supply chain management. In addition, it will assist a researcher in clearing up any respondent doubts that may arise. A systematic questionnaire is employed in the survey procedure. To acquire structured data, the researcher created a formal questionnaire and asked questions in a predetermined order.

3.4.1.3 Sample Size

The below-mentioned formula is used to determine the sample size (Nargundkar,2003).

n= p (1-p) * (z/e) 2

In the above formula,
n= Sample size
p= Frequency of occurrence of something expressed as a proportion,

here p=0.50 **z (Confidence Level)** = Z is the Value associated with confidence level from the standard normal distribution. In simple terms, the Confidence level can be defined as the probability that a confidence interval will include the population parameter. **For this study, the researcher has taken a 95% confidence level (Here from the standard distribution level, the z value is 1.96) based on previous studies.**

e= e is the level of precision that is the tolerance level. Here, the researcher has assumed a tolerance error of 0.05. So here,

N = 0.5 (1-0.5) (1.96/0.05) 2

= 0.25 (1536.64)

= 384

According to the formula, the sample size should be 384. Here, the researcher has taken 424 sample sizes for the current study which is sufficient concerning the formula.

3.5 Research Instrument

A structured questionnaire has been developed to investigate the impact of the green supply chain on the performance of manufacturing units in Gujarat. The questionnaire comprises only closed-ended questions, and a five-point Likert scale is utilized to measure the effect of a green supply chain. The Likert scale is a non-comparative scaling technique that employs itemized scales. The questionnaire has been created using the Likert scale.

3.6 Sampling Technique

The two primary types of sampling methods are probability sampling and non-probability sampling. For the present study, the convenience sampling technique was selected from the non-probability sampling category. This approach was chosen because the researcher intends to evaluate the level of awareness regarding green supply chain management, and respondents will be selected based on their convenience, even though they must have implemented green supply chain practices at their manufacturing firm. The key factors in determining the sample selection were the researcher's judgment, the respondents' convenience, and their willingness to participate.

3.7 Questionnaire Review

The questionnaire was initially reviewed by five experienced academicians. This process has resulted in minor amendments to the wording and sequencing of some Likert scale items.

3.8 Sampling Plan

An extensive survey was carried out to test the hypothesis across manufacturing firms in Gujarat. Respondents selected were CEO/ CFO/ Managers/ Head of the departments as they are closely working to implement a green supply chain, additionally they know the organizational process at 360 degrees. 544 manufacturing firms having green supply chain practices across Gujarat were identified and targeted based on referencing and screening methods based on websites and directories. At least 250 responses are considered testable samples (Hair, Anderson, and Black, 1992), and as per the formula, the sample size should be 384. Thus, the final sample size was 424 which was statistically suitable. Collected data was coded in MS Excel and exported to SPSS and AMOS for further statistical tests. Directories such as INDEXTB and India Brand Equity Foundation (IBEF) from which a list of manufacturing companies was derived. The companies were contacted through personal contacts, website sources, and references.

To conduct the analysis, the researcher employed SPSS and AMOS software. The analysis was divided into two categories, namely descriptive statistics and inferential statistics. Basic descriptive statistics were employed for the former, while Cronbach's Alpha (to evaluate the data's reliability), structural analysis, and measurement models were utilized for the latter in SPSS 22 (Statistical Package for Social Science) and AMOS (Analysis of a Moment Structures).

3.9 Response Rate

A total of 544 companies were identified focusing upon green manufacturing practices across Gujarat. The response rate achieved was 78% i.e. 424 respondents have responded across organisations having green manufacturing practices. The manufacturing organizations were identified based on an in-depth analysis of the website and references received from respondents. According to Ogier (2006), Nulty (2008), and Fryrear (2015), a response rate of 30% is acceptable and desirable.

3.10 Data Collection Plan and Data Analysis

3.10.1 Secondary Data

The term "secondary data" pertains to information that was originally collected for a purpose other than the present research question. To gain a better understanding of the research topic, develop a theoretical framework, and formulate hypotheses, various published sources were considered. Information was gathered from published sources such as thesis/ dissertation, books, magazines, journals, research papers, newspapers, reports, conference proceedings, and reports published by various government sources and private research firms to gain insight into the research field and to develop the theoretical framework and hypotheses. Official speeches and lectures are also utilized as secondary data sources. Secondary data is gathered through online databases (computerized full-text databases) such as ProQuest, Emerald, Sage, SSRN, Google Scholar, and numerous other websites.

3.10.2 Primary Data

Primary data refers to information that is collected by a researcher for the specific purpose of addressing the research problem. In this study, the manufacturing companies taking part in the GSCM provide the primary data. The total sample size for the primary data collection was 424. Primary data can be broadly categorized into two types: qualitative and quantitative. Quantitative data was collected through the structured questionnaire mentioned above. The companies were contacted through personal contacts, website sources, and references. It's a blend of different contact methods.

3.11 Constructs Used in the Study

Sr. No	Name of Construct
1	Green Logistics
2	Institutional Pressure
3	Social Performance
4	Operational performance
5	Green Purchase

Sr. No	Name of Construct
6	Environmental Orientation
7	Normative Pressure
8	Financial Performance
9	Environmental Performance
10	Green Inclination
11	Green Products
12	Green Techno Marketing

3.12 Instrument Development and Scales Measurement

A Questionnaire was developed to get responses to "Research Study based on Green Supply chain practices in Industries of Gujarat". The purpose of the research instrument is to fulfill the research objectives by measuring the dependent and independent variables.

3.13 Pre-testing of the Questionnaire

The primary objective of pre-testing is to evaluate the respondents' capacity to comfortably answer all the questions and eliminate any ambiguous questions. It also helps to ensure that the time required to complete the questionnaire is not excessive and enables researchers to determine the extent to which participants can provide the desired information. In the present study, the researcher designed the questionnaire and discussed its content, format, and variables with a guide. Following the discussion, the questionnaire was modified as necessary. To assess the feasibility of the study and the appropriateness of the instruments employed, a pilot study was conducted with 100 respondents. Cronbach's alpha was used to determine the reliability of the study, and modifications were made to certain questions based on feedback from participants. Furthermore, some of the wording in the questions was altered to make them more easily understandable. It should be noted that the responses gathered during the pilot study were not used for the final data analysis.

3.13.1 Analysis of Pilot Survey

Sr. No.	Constructs	No. of Statements	Cronbach's Alpha
1	Green Logistics	10	0.861
2	Institutional Pressure	6	0.767
3	Social Performance	6	0.889
4	Operational performance	5	0.785
5	Green Purchase	8	0.908
6	Environmental Orientation	9	0.899

Sr. No.	Constructs	No. of Statements	Cronbach's Alpha
7	Normative Pressure	13	0.837
8	Financial Performance	7	0.872
9	Environmental Performance	7	0.867
10	Green Inclination	11	0.843
11	Green Products	8	0.891
12	Green Techno Marketing	9	0.839
13	Awareness	7	0.712
	Total	106	

Here in all the cases, Cronbach's Alpha value is more than 0.7 so it can be said that the data is reliable.

3.13.2 Table

Objectives	Analysis/tools	Achievements
1. To measure awareness of GSCM practices amongst manufacturing firms of Gujarat.	**Descriptive Statistics (Mean & Std Deviation)**	**Various factors measure the awareness of GSCM were identified,**
2. To identify GSCM practices adopted by the selected companies of Gujarat.	**Structural Equation Modelling (SPSS, AMOS)**	**Relationships between the drivers leading toward GSCM practices were identified.**
3. To investigate the impact of the Adoption of GSCM practices on organizational performance	**Structural Equation Modeling (SPSS, AMOS)**	**The linkage between the GSCM practices and Performances was established.**

From the 106 statements, 57 statements were significantly loaded after performing Factor loading on the model, the final statements are as follows:

No	Construct & Statement	Authors
	Institutional Pressure	Diabat, Govindan, & Kannan, (2017) Chen, Geng, Fujita, & Zhu, (2014)
1.	IP1 The regular government examination is carried out which leads our organization to comply with environmental regulations and laws	
2.	IP2 Constant audits are done by organizations for compliance with environmental regulations and laws	Klassen and Vereecke, (2012); Yu, W., Ramanathan, R., (2015);
3.	IP4 By adopting Green Supply Chain Management there is safety assurance for my organization from future legislation of the government	

No	Construct & Statement	Authors
	Normative Pressure	Zhu, Jinyu, (2022); Kalpande, S. D.; Toke, Lalit K., (2021)
4.	NP1 The upward set-up of supply chain supplier to manufacture encouraging my organization to adopt the green initiative	
5.	NP2 Applying best environmental practices leads to increased market share	
6.	NP3 Customers' preference for green products encourages my organization to take green initiatives	
	Environmental Orientation	Muhammad et. al. (2018); Jansson, Marell, & Nordlund (2011); Epstein & Roy (2001); Russo & Fouts (1997); Hobson, Burke, & Pearse,(2006)
7.	EO1 The fundamental corporate value of the organization is the safeguarded environment encourages GSCM adoption	
8.	EO2 The continuous support of senior managers and top-level management motivates for implementation of GSCM	
9.	EO3 Top-level management dedication towards the application of green supply chain management within the organization leads to apply the best environmental policy	
	Green Design	Lenox et al, Linton and Johnson (2000); Thierry et al. (1995); Krikke et al. (1999); Linton and Johnson (2000); Dengelico & Pujari(2021); Goglio et al(2021);
10.	GD1 My Organization has framed a proper structure of the standardized design of our products for reducing energy consumption	
11.	GD2 My Organization has framed a proper structure of the standardized design of our products for reducing the difficulty in processing	
12.	GD3 My organization follows a recyclable design that attains maximum reuse of component	
	Green Purchase	Prates,Glaucia Aparecida (2018); Burritt et al (2011); Pazirandeh and Jafari (2013); Dorigotov et al., (2021); Zhu, Q., Sarkis, J., Lai, K(2008); Sharma et al (2021)
13.	GP1 Issues related to the procurement of material ensure the positive impact by the human health organization	
14.	GP2 Raw material purchased show not be detrimental to the environment is the major factor considered by my organization	
15.	GP3 My organization has adopted a formal approach towards green purchasing or green procurement.	
16.	GP4 My organization is always adapting just-in-time logistic systems for supplier cooperation	
	Green Manufacturing	Acri, Alberto (2022); De Fazio et al. (1997); Johnson (1998); Tan et al. (2002); Ashayeri et al. (1996); Barthorpe (1995);
17.	GM1 An appropriate budget allocation for the application of GSCM practices is done by the organization	
18.	GM2 In process design implementation environmental & efficiency criteria are integrated by my organization	

No	Construct & Statement	Authors
19.	GM3 Minimizes hazardous /toxic waste during manufacturing is always the priority of my organization	
20.	GM4 Environmental factors are taken into consideration while the selection of manufacturing process by my organization	
	Organizational Involvement	Gifford & Nilsson (2014); De Groot & Steg (2018); Kim & Lee (2018)
21.	OI1 The continuous support of senior managers and top-level management ensures for implementation of GSCM	
22.	OI2 Cross-functional cooperation of employees of several departments of my organization encourages to implement of GSCM	
23.	OI3 At our organization efforts are made to establish a linkage between environmental objectives with our companies' corporate goals.	
	Green Marketing	Pujari & Wright (1996); Chen (2008); Lai et al., (2003); Rettie et al (2014); Zhang& Liu (2021); Rana et al., (2021);
24.	GNM1 The eco-labeling /eco-logo is put into operation by my organization	
25.	GNM2 Eco-friendly packaging and eco-friendly aspect relating to the advertisement of the product are mainly considered on a priority base by my organization.	
26.	GNM3 Environmental information is communicated to customers while performing marketing activities	
	Green Distribution	Bulent Sezen (2018); Li et al (2021); Govindan, Kleyner& Stavins (2018); Kumar, Scheibe, & Weber (2020)
27.	GND1 My organization follows a proper procedure to manage all activities to eliminate/reduce environmental waste and damage during shipment	
28.	GND2 My organization's in-vehicle use Eco-Friendly refrigerants	
29.	GND3 In my organization operation of transport vehicles is done by giving importance to fuel efficiency	
	Reverse Logistics	Yalabik et al. (2005); Krikke et al. (1998); Ferrer and Whybark (2000); Dekker et al. (2004); Mirchandani and Francis (1989); Louwers et al (1999)
30.	RL1 My organization makes sure that it's purchased products that must contain green attributes such as recycled or reusable items.	
31.	RL2 Recycling program for manufacturing operation is included by my organization	
32.	RL3 Reverse logistics program is applied in stock planning by my organization	
33.	RL4 Recycling is being considered an essential part by the manufacturers for sustainability management	

No	Construct & Statement	Authors
	Customer Co-Operation	Deleep B (2020); Parast & Shekarian (2019); Verfuerth et al, (2018); Luchs et al (2010)
34.	CC1 My organization considers customers' preferences for products advanced in the environmental record.	
35.	CC2 My organization gives priority to the production of green products considering customers want	
36.	CC3 Regular review of customers is collected to enhance product according to the need of the customer	
37.	CC4 Establishment of social conduct is done for the health and safety of customers	
	Green Technology	Yoo& Gretzel (2021); Hultman& Luchus (2021); Peattie (1995); Polonsky (2005); Mostafa(2007)
38.	GT1 Green technology is cost-effective so more emphasis is given by my organization to the adoption	
39.	GT2 Technology advancement for the manufacturing process is always regarded as vital by my organization.	
40.	GT3 My organization considers it important to adopt Green technology as it plays a vital role in reducing energy consumption	
	Environmental Performance	Hooker, Seckin Ozkul (2019); Eltayeb et al (2011); Chandra Shukla, A.; Deshmukh, S.; Kanda (2009):
41.	EP1 GSCM application results in to decrease in solid waste	
42.	EP2 GSCM application results in to decrease in air emission	
43.	EP3 GSCM application results in to decrease in water wastage	
44.	EP4 GSCM application results in to decrease in releasing harmful pollutants	
	Financial Performance	Joseph Sarkis (2013); Yubing you (2020); Pagell& Shevchenko (2014); Ahi& Searcy (2013)
45.	FP1 GSCM application results in to decrease in penalty for Environmental accidents	
46.	FP2 GSCM application has increased the sales growth of our company	
47.	FP3 GSCM application decreases the cost of capital	
48.	FP4 GSCM application has increased the market share of our company	
49.	FP5 GSCM application has increased earning per share rate of our company	
	Operational Performance	Wantao Yu, Roberto Chavez, Mengying Feng, Frank Wiengarten (2014); Hotlan Siagian(2022); Prajwal Eachempati (2022); S. Lee, J. Sung, D. Choi & Y. Noh, (2013)
50.	OP1 GSCM application increases the number of goods delivered on Time	
51.	OP2 GSCM application results in the reduction of the cost of energy usage	

No	Construct & Statement	Authors
52.	OP3 GSCM application results in a reduction of the scarp	
53.	OP4 GSCM application results in enhancing the quality	
	Social Performance	Zhaojun Han, Baofeng Huo (2020); Jing Wang, Jun Dai (2018); Carter& Rogers, (2008); Sarkis et al., Zhu, & Lai (2011)
54.	SP1 GSCM application helps in improvement in compliance related to the environment	
55.	SP2 GSCM application increases corporate image	
56.	SP3 GSCM application helps organizations for the fulfillment of cooperate social responsibility	
57.	SP4 GSCM application increases social image	

3.14 Proposed Hypotheses

Sr. No	Hypotheses
1	**H_0**: There is no significant impact of **Environmental Orientation** on green inclination
2	**H_0**: There is no significant impact of Environmental Orientation on Green Logistics
3	**H_0**: There is no significant impact of Environmental Orientation on green Techno Marketing
4	**H_0**: There is no significant impact of Environmental Orientation on green Purchase
5	**H_0**: There is no significant impact of **normative pressure** on green inclination
6	**H_0**: There is no significant impact of normative pressure on green Logistics
7	**H_0**: There is no significant impact of normative pressure on green Techno Marketing
8	**H_0**: There is no significant impact of normative pressure on green Product
9	**H_0**: There is no significant impact of normative pressure on green purchases
10	**H_0**: There is no significant impact of **institutional pressure** on green inclination
11	**H_0**: There is no significant impact of institutional pressure on green Logistics
12	**H_0**: There is no significant impact of institutional pressure on green Techno Marketing
13	**H_0**: There is no significant impact of institutional pressure on green Purchase
14	**H_0**: There is no significant impact of **green logistics** on financial performance
15	**H_0**: There is no significant impact of green logistics on social performance
16	**H_0**: There is no significant impact of green logistics on environmental performance
17	**H_0**: There is no significant impact of green logistics on Operational performance
18	**H_0**: There is no significant impact of **Green Inclination** on financial performance
19	**H_0**: There is no significant impact of Green Inclination on social performance
20	**H_0**: There is no significant impact of Green Inclination on environmental performance
21	**H_0**: There is no significant impact of Green Inclination on Operational performance
22	**H_0**: There is no significant impact of **Green Techno Marketing** on Operational performance
23	**H_0**: There is no significant impact of Green Techno Marketing on environmental performance

Sr. No	Hypotheses
24	**H_0**: There is no significant impact of Green Techno Marketing on social performance
25	**H_0**: There is no significant impact of Green Techno Marketing on financial performance
26	**H_0**: There is no significant impact of **Green purchases** on social performance
27	**H_0**: There is no significant impact of Green purchase on financial performance
28	There is no significant impact of Green purchases on environmental performance
29	**H_0**: There is no significant impact of Green purchase on operational performance
30	**H_0**: There is no significant impact of **Green products** on financial performance
31	**H_0**: There is no significant impact of Green products on social performance
32	**H_0**: There is no significant impact of Green products on environmental performance
33	**H_0**: There is no significant impact of Green products on operational performance

3.15 Conclusion

The research methodology can be concluded as under:-

1. **Universe-** Manufacturing companies having green supply chain practices were considered for the Study concerning Gujarat state.
2. **Sampling Technique-** Convenience Sampling
3. **Sample Size**- 424
4. **Method of data collection-** Personal interview with a structured questionnaire
5. **Software used for data analysis-** SPSS 22, AMOS 22

CHAPTER-4

Data Analysis

4.1 Prelude

The current chapter is presenting the data analysis of the quantitative data thereby focusing on the results and findings of the research based on the analysis of the data.

4.1.1 The Data Analysis is Divided into Two Parts

- Part I: Descriptive Statistics (Tests covered are Frequency Distribution Analysis considering the Mean Test, Standard Deviation, and Reliability test)
- Part II: Structural Equation Model (To find the link and impact between the Green Practices and the Performance of the Organizations)

In this chapter, data analysis covering SPSS and AMOS is employed for the analysis. Descriptive statistics and inferential statistics were used to divide the analysis into two sections. Basic analysis is performed under descriptive statistics, while other statistical tests are applied under inferential statistics. The chapter's first section covered the fundamentals of descriptive analysis. Next, a research model is created. To evaluate the effectiveness of the created model, CFA, and measurement validity were done. Before moving on to further analysis, factor loading, AVE, CR, discriminant validity, content validity, and convergent validity were performed. The SEM model was used.

4.1.2 Mean Tests

The respondents were asked to rate the statements on a 5-point Likert scale, where 1 = "Strongly Disagree", 2= Disagree, 3= Neither Agree nor Disagree, 4= Agree, 5 = "Strongly Agree". Any mean score greater than 3 indicates respondents' agreement towards that particular statement.

It was found that the mean of all initial statements was found to be more than 3 indicating respondents' agreement with the statements. None of the statements was found to have a mean less than 3. The mean and standard deviation of all statements are shown in the below table.

Descriptive Statistics (N=424)

Particulars	Mean	Std. Deviation
GSCM Awareness		
M1 Estimated advantage and consciousness of green supply chain management practices encourages my organization to apply GSCM	3.78	.828
M2 Rising in new business opportunities after the application of green supply chain management encourages my organization to follow green practices	3.82	.734
M3 Awareness about GSCM plays a vital role in enhancing both existing and new employees in my organization	3.79	.810
M4 Advancement in technology makes my organization adopt green practices	3.88	.930
M5 Initiatives are made towards rectification of issues related to the implementation of Green practices	3.75	1.073
M6 Attention for promotion of Internet + Green manufacturing encourages to adopt GSCM	3.67	1.012
M7 Social awareness or publicizing the initiative of the company doing a favor to society motivates my organization toward GSCM adoption	3.93	.968
Institutional Pressure		
IP1 The regular government examination is carried out which leads our organization to comply with environmental regulations and laws	4.08	2.114
IP2 Constant audits are done by organizations for compliance with environmental regulations and laws	4.15	2.060
IP3 By adopting Green Supply Chain Management there is safety assurance for my organization from current legislation of the government	3.90	.824
IP4 By adopting Green Supply Chain Management there is safety assurance for my organization from future legislation of the government	4.11	2.026
IP5 Taxes for environment protection leads towards implementation of green practices	3.06	1.314
IP6 Enforcement of law for environment protection leads towards implementation of green practices	3.75	.980
Normative Pressure		
NP1 The upward set-up of supply chain supplier to manufacture encouraging my organization to adopt a green initiative	4.12	2.043
NP2 Applying best environmental practices leads to increased market share	3.99	2.057
NP3 Customers' preference for green products encourages my organization to take green initiatives	4.06	2.047
NP4 Customers are considered strategic partners for collaboration on green issues	3.82	.914
NP5 Export Market has an eminent role in the adoption of Green Practices	3.67	1.497
NP6 The market demand plays an enormous role in the adoption of Green Practices	3.82	.857

Particulars	Mean	Std. Deviation
NP7 Awareness about the eco-design of the product motives my organization towards adoption of GSCM	3.83	.744
NP8 Demand of customers for eco-design products encourages them to adopt Green practices	3.89	.884
NP9 Cooperation of a customer for a clean environment leads to adopting GSCM	3.90	.897
NP10 Consumers' Preference for Environmental Consideration makes the organization adopt GSCM	3.73	.981
NP11 Audit of Supplier is leading for considering sustainability management	3.88	.869
NP12 Collaboration with supplier for environmental sustainability leads promotes GSCM	3.79	.881
NP13 Sharing responsibilities with suppliers encourages them to adopt more environmentally friendly behaviors	3.70	.668
Environmental Orientation		
EO1 The fundamental corporate value of the organization is the safeguarded environment encourages GSCM adoption	4.13	2.054
EO2 The continuous support of senior managers and top-level management motivates for implementation of GSCM	4.08	2.023
EO3 Top-level management dedication towards the application of green supply chain management within the organization leads to apply the best environmental policy	4.12	2.121
EO4 Organizational process which is designed to minimize the use of Restriction of Hazardous Substances assures reduction of adverse environmental effects is achieved and encourages the adoption of GSCM	3.83	.953
EO5 The Corporate Social responsibility encourages adopting GSCM	3.73	.849
EO6 Priority of selecting those practices which involve environmental criteria encourages GSCM adoption	3.87	.858
EO7 Adopting Green manufacturing activity increases the efficiency of my organization and motivates my organization to follow GSCM practices	3.82	.923
EO8 Policy of designing products in recyclable form has involved my company in going for GSCM	3.91	.865
EO9 Organization's one-part accountability for processes related to environmental standards leads to following best green practices	3.84	.660
Green Design		
GD1 My Organization has framed a proper structure of the standardized design of our products for reducing energy consumption	4.08	2.084
GD2 My Organization has framed a proper structure of the standardized design of our products for reducing the difficulty in processing	4.18	2.016
GD3 My organization follows a recyclable design that attains maximum reuse of component	4.05	2.118

Particulars	Mean	Std. Deviation
Green Purchase		
GP1 Issues related to the procurement of material ensure the positive impact by the human health organization	4.04	1.982
GP2 Raw material purchased show not be detrimental to the environment is the major factor considered by my organization	4.08	1.996
GP3 My organization has adopted a formal approach towards green purchasing or green procurement.	4.14	2.028
GP4 My organization is always adapting just-in-time logistic systems for supplier cooperation	4.09	2.047
GP5 My organization requires its suppliers to develop and maintain an EMS and encourage suppliers with certified EMS such as ISO 14001.	3.73	.951
GP6 My organization follow proper Quality check to produce the raw material	3.73	.836
GP7 Initiative is taken by my organization to organize workshops/seminars to educate our suppliers GSCM	3.89	.834
GP8 Selection of suppliers is done based on their performance through formal evaluation, using established guidelines and procedures for GSCM.	3.79	.979
Green Manufacturing		
GM1 An appropriate budget allocation for the application of GSCM practices is done by an organization	4.07	2.065
GM2 In process design implementation environmental & efficiency criteria are integrated by my organization	4.14	2.024
GM3 Minimizes hazardous /toxic waste during manufacturing is always the priority of my organization	4.07	2.084
GM4 Environmental factors are taken into consideration while selecting manufacturing process by my organization	4.12	1.997
GM5 Environmental factors are considered while planning production and control by my organization.	3.90	.791
Organizational Involvement		
OI1 The continuous support of senior managers and top-level management ensures for implementation of GSCM	4.11	2.072
OI2 Cross-functional cooperation of employees of several departments of my organization encourages to implement of GSCM	4.06	2.068
OI3 At our organization efforts are made to establish a linkage between environmental objectives with our companies' corporate goals.	4.09	2.094
OI4 There is encouragement for departmental interaction and exchange of information concerning activities like performance, environment, efficiency, and many more	3.62	.900

Particulars	Mean	Std. Deviation
Green Marketing		
GNM1 The eco-labeling/eco-logo is put into operation by my organization	4.01	2.112
GNM2 Eco-friendly packaging and eco-friendly aspect relating to the advertisement of the product are mainly considered on a priority base by my organization.	4.02	2.092
GNM3 Environmental information is communicated to customers while performing marketing activities	4.06	1.984
GNM4 Green marketing encourages increasing profit of the business	3.14	1.269
Green Distribution		
GND1 My organization follows a proper procedure to manage all activities to eliminate/reduce environmental waste and damage during shipment	4.11	2.087
GND2 My organization's in-vehicle uses Eco-Friendly refrigerants	4.04	2.036
GND3 In my organization operation of transport vehicles is done by giving importance to fuel efficiency	4.15	2.014
Reverse Logistics		
RL1 My organization makes sure that it's purchased products that must contain green attributes such as recycled or reusable items.	4.04	2.072
RL2 Recycling program for manufacturing operation is included by my organization	4.08	2.164
RL3 Reverse logistics program is applied in stock planning by my organization	4.03	2.054
RL4 Recycling is being considered an essential part by the manufacturers for sustainability management	4.09	2.006
RL5 Policy of taking back packaging has involved companies going for GSCM	3.29	1.106
RL6 Trend of consideration of the end life of the company's product has increased due to GSCM	3.79	1.232
RL7 My organization recovers products and/or components from customers for repair and remanufacture.	3.22	1.169
Customer Co-Operation		
CC1 My organization considers customers' preferences for products advanced in the environmental record.	4.05	2.111
CC2 My organization gives priority to the production of green products considering customers want	3.99	2.034
CC3 Regular review of customers is collected to enhance product according to the need of the customer	4.11	2.116
CC4 Establishment of social conduct is done for the health and safety of customers	4.14	2.076
CC5 My organization gets a good amount of cooperation from the customer for implementing the Eco-design of a product	3.92	.788
CC6 My organization gets a good amount of cooperation from customers for cleaner production	3.64	.924

Particulars	Mean	Std. Deviation
CC7 My organization gets a good amount of cooperation from customers for green purchasing	3.85	.865
Green Technology		
GT1 Green technology is cost-effective so more emphasis is given by my organization to the adoption	4.07	2.028
GT2 Technology advancement for the manufacturing process is always regarded vital by my organization.	4.08	2.040
GT3 My organization considers it important to adopt Green technology as it plays a vital role in reducing energy consumption	4.07	2.055
GT4 My organization considers important the adoption of green technology as it has less impact on the environment	3.88	.698
GT5 My organization adopts green technology as it helps in practicing innovative power production techniques.	3.79	.959
Environmental Performance		
EP1 GSCM application results in to decrease in solid waste	4.08	2.117
EP2 GSCM application results in to decrease in air emission	4.11	2.136
EP3 GSCM application results in to decrease in water wastage	4.03	2.074
EP4 GSCM application results in to decrease in releasing harmful pollutants	4.16	2.048
EP5 GSCM application results in to increase in Organization's Environmental condition	4.06	1.994
EP6 GSCM application results in to decrease in the utilization of toxic /hazardous/harmful material	3.49	1.096
EP7 GSCM application reduces carbon footprints	3.79	.857
Financial Performance		
FP1 GSCM application results in to decrease in penalty for Environmental accidents	4.08	2.055
FP2 GSCM application has increased the sales growth of our company	4.04	2.108
FP3 GSCM application decreases the cost of capital	4.05	2.058
FP4 GSCM application has increased the market share of our company	4.15	2.109
FP5 GSCM application has increased earning per share rate of our company	3.26	1.510
FP6 GSCM application has reduced the cost of material purchasing	3.14	1.269
FP7 GSCM application has reduced fees for waste discharge	3.32	1.201
Operational Performance		
OP1 GSCM application increases the number of goods delivered on Time	4.03	2.035
OP2 GSCM application results in the reduction of the cost of energy usage	4.08	2.047
OP3 GSCM application results in a reduction of the scarp	3.26	1.806
OP4 GSCM application results in enhancing the quality	4.06	2.044

Particulars	Mean	Std. Deviation
OP5 GSCM application in the reduction of inventory level	3.51	1.078
Social Performance		
SP1 GSCM application helps in improvement in compliance related to the environment	4.05	2.046
SP2 GSCM application increases corporate image	4.09	2.117
SP3 GSCM application helps organizations for the fulfillment of cooperate social responsibility	4.05	2.048
SP4 GSCM application increases social image	4.07	2.049
SP5 GSCM application helps in reducing no environmental accident	3.81	.805
SP6 GSCM application leads in gaining customer loyalty toward the organization	3.68	.935

Variable-wise Mean Tests

1. GSCM Awareness

Statement	Mean	Std. Deviation
M1 Estimated advantage and consciousness of green supply chain management practices encourages my organization to the application of GSCM	3.78	.828
M2 Rising in new business opportunities after the application of green supply chain management encourages my organization to follow green practices	3.82	.734
M3 Awareness of GSCM plays a vital role in enhancing both existing and new employees in my organization	3.79	.810
M4 Advancement in technology makes my organization adopt green practices	3.88	.930
M5 Initiatives are made towards rectification of issues related to the implementation of Green practices	3.75	1.073
M6 Attention for promotion of Internet + Green manufacturing encourages to adopt GSCM	3.67	1.012
M7 Social awareness or publicizing the initiative of the company doing a favor to society motivates my organization toward GSCM adoption	3.93	.968
Valid N (listwise)		

It was found that the mean of 7 initial statements of the GSCM Awareness variable was found to be more than 3 indicating respondents' agreement with the statements. None of the statements was found to have a mean less than 3. The mean and standard deviation of all statements are shown in the above table. It can analyze that bringing social awareness about the initiatives by the company for the welfare of society plays the eminent in adoption of the green practices. Also, the advancement in technology and the rising new business opportunities are the main focal point of awareness.

2. Institutional Pressure

Statement	Mean	Std. Deviation
IP1 The regular government examination is carried out which leads our organization to comply with environmental regulations and laws	4.08	2.114
IP2 Constant audits are done by organizations for compliance with environmental regulations and laws	4.15	2.060
IP3 By adopting Green Supply Chain Management there is safety assurance for my organization from current legislation of the government	3.90	.824
IP4 By adopting Green Supply Chain Management there is safety assurance for my organization from future legislation of the government	4.11	2.026
IP5 Taxes for environment protection leads towards implementation of green practices	3.06	1.314
IP6 Enforcement of law for environment protection leads towards implementation of green practices	3.75	.980

It was found that the mean of 6 initial statements of the Institutional Pressure variable was found to be more than 3 indicating respondents' agreement with the statements. None of the statements was found to have a mean less than 3. The mean and standard deviation of all statements are shown in the above table. It can be analyzed that factors such as safety assurance, constant audits, and regular government examination are the leading factors for Intuitional pressure.

3. Normative Pressure

Statement	Mean	Std. Deviation
NP1 The upward set-up of supply chain supplier to manufacture encouraging my organization to adopt the green initiative	4.12	2.043
NP2 Applying best environmental practices leads to increased market share	3.99	2.057
NP3 Customers' preference for green products encourages my organization to take green initiatives	4.06	2.047
NP4 Customers are considered strategic partners for collaboration on green issues	3.82	.914
NP5 Export Market has an eminent role in the adoption of Green Practices	3.67	1.497
NP6 The market demand plays an enormous role in the adoption of Green Practices	3.82	.857
NP7 Awareness about the eco-design of the product motives my organization towards adoption of GSCM	3.83	.744
NP8 Demand of customers for eco-design products encourages them to adopt Green practices	3.89	.884
NP9 Cooperation of the customer for a clean environment leads to adopting GSCM	3.90	.897
NP10 Consumers' Preference for Environmental Consideration makes the organization adopt GSCM	3.73	.981
NP11 Audit of Supplier is leading for considering sustainability management	3.88	.869

Statement	Mean	Std. Deviation
NP12 Collaboration with supplier for environmental sustainability leads promotes GSCM	3.79	.881
NP13 Sharing responsibilities with suppliers encourages them to adopt more environmentally friendly behaviors	3.70	.668

It was found that the mean of 13 initial statements of the Normative Pressure variable was found to be more than 3 indicating respondents' agreement with the statements. None of the statements was found to have a mean less than 3. The mean and standard deviation of all statements are shown in the above table. From the table, we can analyze factors such as the cooperation of the customer for a clean environment, the demand of customers for eco-design products, customers' preference for green products encourages, the upward set-up of supply chain suppliers to manufacture, market demand, awareness about the eco-design of the product and audit of the supplier are leading ones for Normative Pressure.

4. Environmental Orientation

Statement	Mean	Std. Deviation
EO1 The fundamental corporate value of the organization is the safeguarded environment encourages GSCM adoption	4.13	2.054
EO2 The continuous support of senior managers and top-level management motivates for implementation of GSCM	4.08	2.023
EO3 Top-level management dedication towards the application of green supply chain management within the organization leads to apply the best environmental policy	4.12	2.121
EO4 Organizational process which is designed to minimize the use of Restriction of Hazardous Substances assures reduction of adverse environmental effects is achieved and encourages the adoption of GSCM	3.83	.953
EO5 The Corporate Social responsibility encourages adopting GSCM	3.73	.849
EO6 Priority of selecting those practices which involve environmental criteria encourages GSCM adoption	3.87	.858
EO7 Adopting Green manufacturing activity increases the efficiency of my organization and motivates my organization to follow GSCM practices	3.82	.923
EO8 Policy of designing products in recyclable form has involved my company in going for GSCM	3.91	.865
EO9 Organization's one-part accountability for processes related to environmental standards leads to following best green practices	3.84	.660

It was found that the mean of 9 initial statements of the Environmental Orientation variable was found to be more than 3 indicating respondents' agreement with the statements. None of the statements was found to have a mean less than 3. The mean and standard deviation of all statements are shown in the above table. From the data in the table, it can be analyzed that factors such as the policy of designing products in recyclable form, top-level management dedication towards the application of green supply chain management, the continuous support of senior managers and top- level management, the corporate value of the organization is to safeguard the environment are the leading ones for Environment Orientation.

5. Green Design

Statement	Mean	Std. Deviation
GD1 My Organization has framed a proper structure of the standardized design of our products for reducing energy consumption	4.08	2.084
GD2 My Organization has framed a proper structure of the standardized design of our products for reducing the difficulty in processing	4.18	2.016
GD3 My organization follows a recyclable design that attains maximum reuse of component	4.05	2.118

It was found that the mean of 3 initial statements of the Green Design variable was found to be more than 3 indicating respondents' agreement with the statements. None of the statements was found to have a mean less than 3. The mean and standard deviation of all statements are shown in the above table. From the table, it can be analyzed that proper structure of standardized design considering a reduction in energy consumption, reducing the difficulty in processing, and design that attains maximum reuse of components are the leading ones for adopting Green Design.

6. Green Purchase

Statement	Mean	Std. Deviation
GP1 Issues related to the procurement of material ensure the positive impact by the human health organization	4.04	1.982
GP2 Raw material purchased show not be detrimental to the environment is the major factor considered by my organization	4.08	1.996
GP3 My organization has adopted a formal approach towards green purchasing or green procurement.	4.14	2.028
GP4 My organization is always adapting just-in-time logistic systems for supplier cooperation	4.09	2.047
GP5 My organization requires its suppliers to develop and maintain an EMS and encourage suppliers with certified EMS such as ISO 14001.	3.73	.951
GP6 My organization follow proper Quality check to produce the raw material	3.73	.836
GP7 Initiative is taken by my organization to organize workshops/seminars to educate our suppliers GSCM	3.89	.834
GP8 Selection of suppliers is done based on their performance through formal evaluation, using established guidelines and procedures for GSCM.	3.79	.979

It was found that the mean of 8 initial statements of the Green Purchase variable was found to be more than 3 indicating respondents' agreement with the statements. None of the statements was found to have a mean less than 3. The mean and standard deviation of all statements are shown in the above table. From the table, it can be analyzed that factors such as procurement of materials that is safeguarding human health, adapting just in time logistic system for supplier cooperation, adoption of formal approach towards green purchasing or green procurement

7. Green Manufacturing

Statement	Mean	Std. Deviation
GM1 An appropriate budget allocation for the application of GSCM practices is done by the organization	4.07	2.065
GM2 In process design implementation environmental & efficiency criteria are integrated by my organization	4.14	2.024
GM3 Minimizes hazardous /toxic waste during manufacturing is always the priority of my organization	4.07	2.084
GM4 Environmental factors are taken into consideration while the selection of manufacturing process by my organization	4.12	1.997
GM5 Environmental factors are considered while planning production and control by my organization.	3.90	.791

It was found that the mean of 5 initial statements of the Green Manufacturing variable was found to be more than 3 indicating respondents' agreement with the statements. None of the statements was found to have a mean less than 3. The mean and standard deviation of all statements are shown in the above table. From the table, it can be analyzed that factors such as considering environmental aspects for the selection of manufacturing process, reduction in toxic waste, appropriate budget allocation, and integration of environmental & efficiency criteria in process design are the leading components for adopting Green Manufacturing.

8. Organizational Involvements

Statement	Mean	Std. Deviation
OI1 The continuous support of senior managers and top-level management ensures for implementation of GSCM	4.11	2.072
OI2 Cross-functional cooperation of employees of several departments of my organization encourages to implement GSCM	4.06	2.068
OI3 At our organization efforts are made to establish a linkage between environmental objectives with our companies' corporate goals.	4.09	2.094
OI4 There is encouragement for departmental interaction and exchange of information concerning activities like performance, environment, efficiency, and many more	3.62	.900

It was found that the mean of 4 initial statements of the Organizational Involvement variable was found to be more than 3 indicating respondents' agreement with the statements. None of the statements was found to have a mean less than 3. The mean and standard deviation of all statements are shown in the above table. From the above table, it can be analyzed that factors such as integration of environmental objectives with the company's corporate goals, cross-functional cooperation of employees of several departments, and continuous support of senior managers and top-level management are the main components leading towards the Involvement of the Organization.

9. Green Marketing

Statement	Mean	Std. Deviation
GNM1 The eco-labeling /eco-logo is put into operation by my organization	4.01	2.112
GNM2 Eco-friendly packaging and eco-friendly aspect relating to the advertisement of the product are mainly considered on a priority base by my organization.	4.02	2.092
GNM3 Environmental information is communicated to customers while performing marketing activities	4.06	1.984
GNM4 Green marketing encourages increasing profit of the business	3.14	1.269

It was found that the mean of 4 initial statements of the GREEN MARKETING variable was found to be more than 3 indicating respondents' agreement with the statements. None of the statements was found to have a mean of less than 3. The mean and standard deviation of all statements are shown in the above table. From the above table, it can be analyzed that factors such as eco–labeling/ eco-logo, Eco-friendly packaging, and eco-friendly aspect for advertising and communication of environmental information to the customers are the main components leading towards the adoption of Green Marketing.

10. Green Distribution

Statement	Mean	Std. Deviation
GND1 My organization follows a proper procedure to manage all activities to eliminate/reduce environmental waste and damage during shipment	4.11	2.087
GND2 My organization in a vehicle uses Eco-Friendly refrigerants	4.04	2.036
GND3 In my organization operation of transport vehicles is done by giving importance to fuel efficiency	4.15	2.014

It was found that the mean of 3 initial statements of GSCM practices variable Green Distribution was found to be more than 3 indicating respondents' agreement with the statements. None of the statements was found to have a mean less than 3. The mean and standard deviation of all statements are shown in the above table. From the table, it can be analyzed that factors such as the proper procedure to eliminate/reduce environmental waste and damage, vehicle use of Eco-Friendly refrigerants, and fuel efficiency are the leading factors of Green Distribution that are presenting a positive impact on the application of GSCM.

11. Reverse Logistics

Statement	Mean	Std. Deviation
RL1 My organization makes sure that it's purchased products that must contain green attributes such as recycled or reusable items.	4.04	2.072
RL2 Recycling program for manufacturing operation is included by my organization	4.08	2.164
RL3 Reverse logistics program is applied in stock planning by my organization	4.03	2.054
RL4 Recycling is being considered an essential part by the manufacturers for sustainability management	4.09	2.006
RL5 Policy of taking back packaging has involved companies going for GSCM	3.29	1.106
RL6 Trend of consideration of the end life of the company's product has increased due to GSCM	3.79	1.232
RL7 My organization recovers products and/or components from customers for repair and remanufacture.	3.22	.169

It was found that the mean of 7 initial statements of the REVERSE LOGISTICS variable was found to be more than 3 indicating respondents' agreement with the statements. None of the statements was found to have a mean less than 3. The mean and standard deviation of all statements are shown in the above table. From the above data, it can be analyzed that factors such as green attributes, Recycling Programs, and Reverse Logistics programs are the leading factors that are presenting a positive impact on the application of GSCM.

12. Customer Co-Operation

Statement	Mean	Std. Deviation
CC1 My organization considers customers' preferences for products advanced in the environmental record.	4.05	2.111
CC2 My organization gives priority to the production of green products considering customers want	3.99	2.034
CC3 Regular review of customers is collected to enhance product according to the need of the customer	4.11	2.116
CC4 Establishment of social conduct is done for the health and safety of customers	4.14	2.076
CC5 My organization gets a good amount of cooperation from the customer for implementing the Eco-design of a product	3.92	.788
CC6 My organization gets a good amount of cooperation from customers for cleaner production	3.64	.924
CC7 My organization gets a good amount of cooperation from customers for green purchasing	3.85	.865

It was found that the mean of 7 initial statements of the CUSTOMER CO-OPERATION variable was found to be more than 3 indicating respondents' agreement with the statements. None of the statements was found to have a mean less than 3. The mean and standard deviation of all statements are shown in the above table. From the table, it can be analyzed that factors such as customer preference, review of customers, social conduct, and cooperation from the customer for implementing Eco-design are the leading factors of Customer Cooperation which are presenting a positive impact on the application of GSCM.

13. Green Technology

Statement	Mean	Std. Deviation
GT1 Green technology is so more emphasis is given by my organization for adoption	4.07	2.028
GT2 Technology advancement for the manufacturing process is always regarded as vital by my organization. cost-effective	4.08	2.040
GT3 My organization considers it important to adopt Green technology as it plays a vital role in reducing energy consumption	4.07	2.055
GT4 My organization considers important the adoption of green technology as it has less impact on the environment	3.88	.698
GT5 My organization adopts green technology as it helps in practicing innovative power production techniques.	3.79	.959

It was found that the mean of 5 initial statements of the GREEN TECHNOLOGY variable was found to be more than 3 indicating respondents' agreement with the statements. None of the statements was found to have a mean less than 3. The mean and standard deviation of all statements are shown in the above table. From the table, it can be analyzed that factors such as cost-effectiveness, Technology advancement for the manufacturing process, and adoption of Green Technology are the leading factors that are presenting a positive impact on the application of GSCM.

14. Environmental Performance

Statement	Mean	Std. Deviation
EP1 GSCM application results in to decrease in solid waste	4.08	2.117
EP2 GSCM application results in to decrease in air emission	4.11	2.136
EP3 GSCM application results in to decrease in water wastage	4.03	2.074
EP4 GSCM application results in to decrease in releasing harmful pollutants	4.16	2.048
EP5 GSCM application results in to increase in the Organization's Environmental condition	4.06	1.994
EP6 GSCM application results in to decrease in the utilization of toxic/hazardous/ harmful material	3.49	1.096
EP7 GSCM application reduces carbon footprints	3.79	.857

It was found that the mean of 7 initial statements of the ENVIRONMENTAL PERFORMANCE variable was found to be more than 3 indicating respondents' agreement with the statements. None of the statements was found to have a mean of less than 3. The mean and standard deviation of all statements are shown in the above table. From the above table, it can be analyzed that a decrease in solid waste, a decrease in air emissions, a decrease in water wastage, a decrease in releasing harmful pollutants, and an increase in the Organization's environmental condition are the leading factors of Environmental Performance which are showing presenting positive impact on the application of GSCM.

15. Financial Performances

Statement	Mean	Std. Deviation
FP1 GSCM application results in to decrease in penalty for Environmental accidents	4.08	2.055
FP2 GSCM application has increased the sales growth of our company	4.04	2.108
FP3 GSCM application decreases the cost of capital	4.05	2.058
FP4 GSCM application has increased the market share of our company	4.15	2.109
FP5 GSCM application has increased earning per share rate of our company	3.26	1.510
FP6 GSCM application has reduced the cost of material purchasing	3.14	1.269
FP7 GSCM application has reduced fees for waste discharge	3.32	1.201

It was found that the mean of 7 initial statements of the FINANCIAL PERFORMANCE variable was found to be more than 3 indicating respondents' agreement with the statements. None of the statements was found to have a mean of less than 3. The mean and standard deviation of all statements are shown in the above table. From the above data it can be analysed that a decrease in penalties for Environmental accidents, sales growth, decreases cost of capital, and increase market share are leading factors of the financial performance which are showing that positive impact towards the application of the GSCM.

16. Operational Performance

Statement	Mean	Std. Deviation
OP1 GSCM application increases the quantity of goods delivered on Time	4.03	2.035
OP2 GSCM application results in a reduction of cost of energy usage	4.08	2.047
OP3 GSCM application results in a reduction of a scarp	3.26	1.806
OP4 GSCM application results in enhancing the quality	4.06	2.044
OP5 GSCM application in the reduction of inventory level	3.51	1.078

It was found that the mean of 5 initial statements of the OPERATIONAL PERFORMANCE variable was found to be more than 3 indicating respondents' agreement with the statements. None of the statements was found to have a mean of less than 3. The mean and standard deviation of all statements are shown in the above table. From the above table, it can be analyzed that factors such as an increase in the quantity of goods delivery, reduction of cost of energy, and enhancement in quality are the of the operational performance which is leading towards the green supply chain management.

17. Social Performance

Statement	Mean	Std. Deviation
SP1 GSCM application helps in improvement in compliance related to the environment	4.05	2.046
SP2 GSCM application increases corporate image	4.09	2.117
SP3 GSCM application helps organizations for fulfillment of cooperate social responsibility	4.05	2.048
SP4 GSCM application increases social image	4.07	2.049
SP5 GSCM application helps in reducing no environmental accident	3.81	.805
SP6 GSCM application leads in gaining customer loyalty toward the organization	3.68	.935

It was found that the mean of 6 initial statements of the SOCIAL PERFORMANCE variable was found to be more than 3 indicating respondents' agreement with the statements. None of the statements was found to have a mean of less than 3. The mean and standard deviation of all statements are shown in the above table. From the table it can be analysed that the rising of social image, improvement in compliance, fulfilment of cooperate social responsibility, increases corporate image, and improvement in compliance are the main components of the social performance that are leading towards the application of GSCM.

4.1.3 Reliability Analysis – Cronbach's Alpha

In statistics and psychometrics, a measure's dependability is its overall consistency. If a metric continually yields the same findings, it is seen as more reliable. Cronbach's alpha was used to evaluate reliability. An alpha value better than 0.70 is considered to be an excellent measure of internal consistency by Nunnally (1978). It was discovered that the construct alpha values consistently surpassed the norm. The alpha values were discovered to be 0.955. As a result, variables with alpha values larger than 0.7 had exceptionally high levels of reliability which indicates data is reliable for further testing.

Reliability Statistics	
Cronbach's Alpha	N of Items
.996	56

4.1.4 Frequency Analysis

1. Awareness

Are you aware of the concept of "Green Supply Chain Management"?

1. Yes
2. No

Awareness	Frequency	Percent
Yes	424	100.0

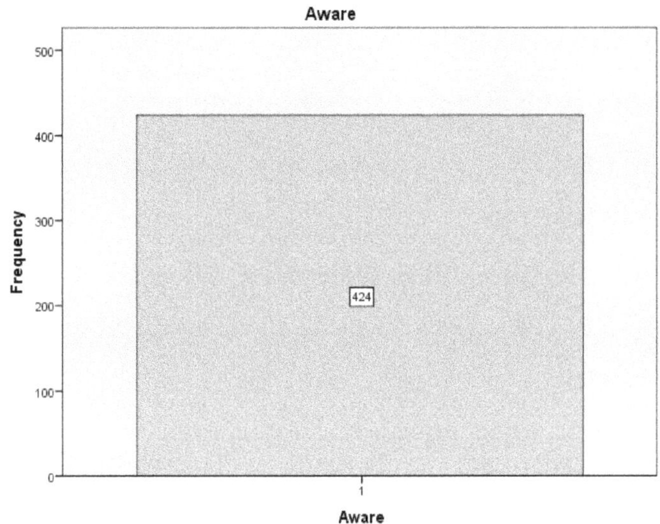

Interpretation: The researcher found that all 424 respondents are aware of the concept of "Green Supply Chain Management".

2. Implementation

Is there any implementation of Green Supply Chain Management Practices in your Organization?

1. Yes
2. No

Implementation	Frequency	Percent
Yes	424	100.0

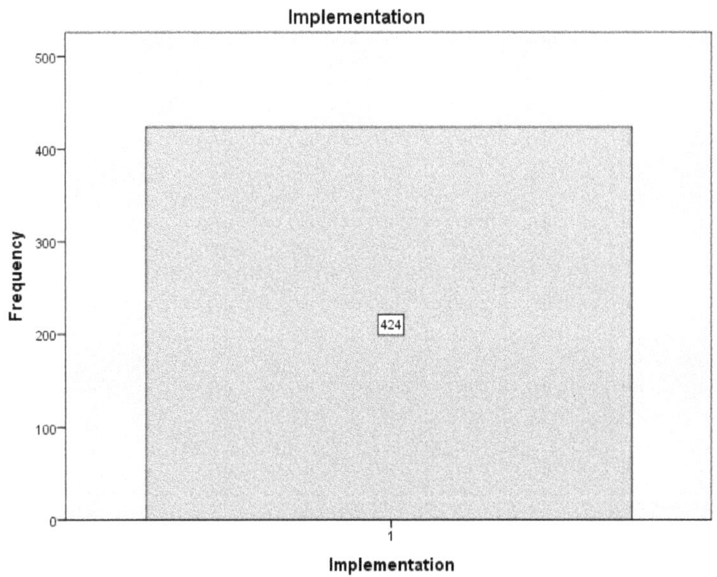

As per the above analysis, we can see that all the respondents' organizations have implemented green supply chains. Manufacturing firms who have implemented green supply chain practices are considered for the study.

3. Stage

Stage of Implementation of Green Supply Chain Management in my organization

1. Advanced Stage (Fully applied and reported Authorized Sustainability Statement, Adopted practice from more than 5 years)
2. Middle Stage (Authorized Sustainability Statement, Adopted practice from 2 year-5 years)
3. Initial stage (Authorized Sustainability Statement, Adopted practice from 1 year-2 years)
4. Emergence Stage

Serial No	Stages	Frequency	Percent	Cumulative Percent
1.	Advanced	19	4.5	4.5
2.	Middle	71	16.7	21.2
3.	Initial	180	42.5	63.7
4.	Emergence	154	36.3	100.0
	Total	424	100.0	

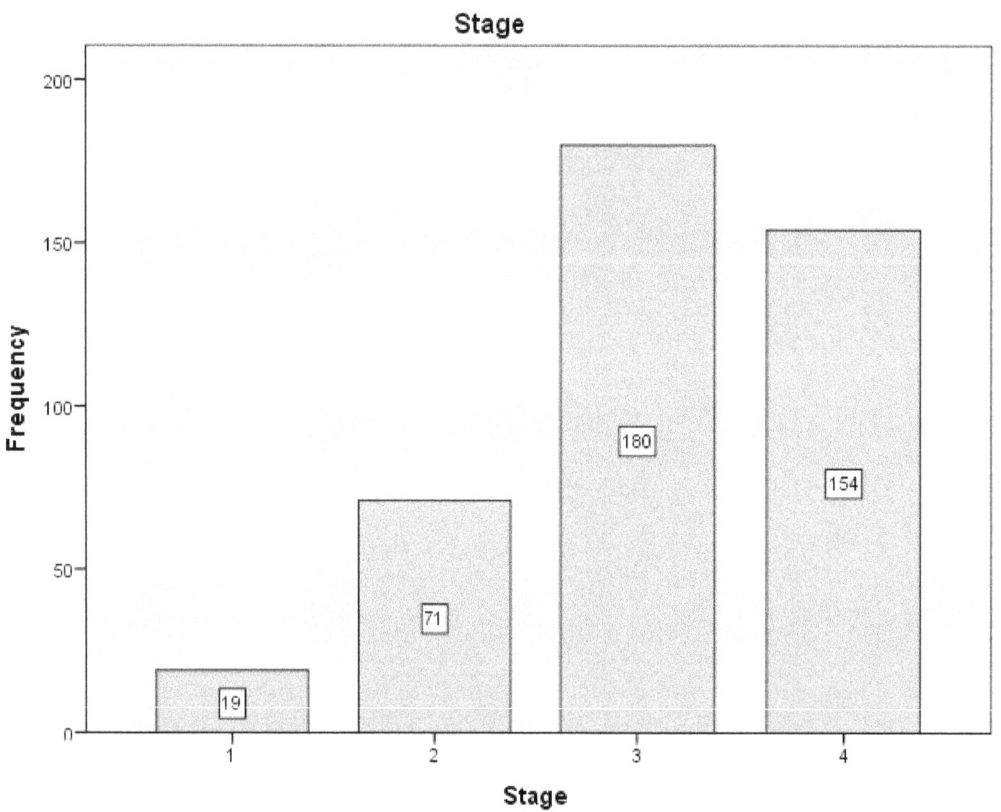

From the about table, it can be observed that 4.5% of respondents' organizations are in the Advanced stage, 16.7% are in the Middle stage, 42.5% are in the Initial stage which is the majority, whereas 36.3% are in the Emergence stage.

The frequency distribution table displays awareness statements and their frequencies

M1 Estimated advantage and consciousness of green supply chain management practices encourages my organization to apply of GSCM

No.		Frequency	Percent	Valid Percent	Cumulative Percent
Valid	1	5	1.2	1.2	1.2
	2	4	.9	.9	2.1
	3	161	38.0	38.0	40.1
	4	165	38.9	38.9	79.0
	5	89	21.0	21.0	100.0
	Total	424	100.0	100.0	

M2 Rising in new business opportunities after the application of green supply chain management encourages my organization to follow green practices

		Frequency	Percent	Valid Percent	Cumulative Percent
Valid	2	3	.7	.7	.7
	3	151	35.6	35.6	36.3
	4	191	45.0	45.0	81.4
	5	79	18.6	18.6	100.0
	Total	424	100.0	100.0	

M3 Awareness of GSCM plays a vital role in enhancing both existing and new employees in my organization

		Frequency	Percent	Valid Percent	Cumulative Percent
Valid	1	4	.9	.9	.9
	2	3	.7	.7	1.7
	3	161	38.0	38.0	39.6
	4	168	39.6	39.6	79.2
	5	88	20.8	20.8	100.0
	Total	424	100.0	100.0	

M4 Advancement in technology makes my organization adopt green practices

		Frequency	Percent	Valid Percent	Cumulative Percent
Valid	1	8	1.9	1.9	1.9
	2	4	.9	.9	2.8
	3	152	35.8	35.8	38.7
	4	128	30.2	30.2	68.9
	5	132	31.1	31.1	100.0
	Total	424	100.0	100.0	

M5 Initiatives are made towards rectification of issues related to the implementation of Green practices

		Frequency	Percent	Valid Percent	Cumulative Percent
Valid	1	23	5.4	5.4	5.4
	2	14	3.3	3.3	8.7
	3	129	30.4	30.4	39.2
	4	137	32.3	32.3	71.5
	5	121	28.5	28.5	100.0
	Total	424	100.0	100.0	

M6 Attention for promotion of Internet + Green manufacturing encourages to adopt GSCM

		Frequency	Percent	Valid Percent	Cumulative Percent
Valid	1	22	5.2	5.2	5.2
	2	15	3.5	3.5	8.7
	3	131	30.9	30.9	39.6
	4	167	39.4	39.4	79.0
	5	89	21.0	21.0	100.0
	Total	424	100.0	100.0	

M7 Social awareness or publicizing the initiative of a company doing a favour to society motivates my organization towards GSCM adoption

		Frequency	Percent	Valid Percent	Cumulative Percent
Valid	1	11	2.6	2.6	2.6
	2	9	2.1	2.1	4.7
	3	122	28.8	28.8	33.5
	4	140	33.0	33.0	66.5
	5	142	33.5	33.5	100.0
	Total	424	100.0	100.0	

Interpretation

The above analysis concludes that all the Companies are aware of green practices. Awareness has increased as a green supply chain gives firms an opportunity in terms of business expansion and growth. Mostly the frequencies of responses are for Strongly Agree and Agree. Hence it can be concluded from the frequency table that key aspects such as consciousness of green supply chain management practices, rising in new business opportunities after the application of green supply chain management, and Enhancement of employees on the adoption of GSCM leads to generating awareness among the organization for GSCM. Additionally, many firms have adopted green supply chain practices considering the advanced technology also as a vital factor for awareness of GSCM. Furthermore, firms are aware that, green supply chain practices will benefit them in high social awareness and will generate greater publicity thereby directing them towards the adoption of GSCM.

4.2 AMOS

4.2.1 Confirmatory Factor Analysis

The data from the survey are analyzed using structural equation modeling (SEM). There are several advantages to comparing SEM to more conventional methods of analysis, such as running multiple regressions on each dependent variable in the model. SEM can be employed as a confirmatory factor analysis tool to assess the dimensionality and validity of each construct (Kline 1998). This analytical tool may also analyze a system of posited equations with several dependent variables simultaneously (Singh 1995). SEM allows researchers to account for measurement error for each model construct and evaluate the effectiveness of the model as a whole by providing multivariate goodness-of-fit indices (Hair et al. 1992). Additionally, it permits a thorough examination of potential model modifications and a comparison of the suggested model with other similar and constrained models (Kline 1998).

4.2.2 Measurement Model

Confirmatory factor analysis (CFA) was used on the constructions to show that the manifest variables load upon and are indicative of the recommended constructs. The researcher can use CFA and construct validity tests to evaluate the accuracy of their measures inside a measurement model before evaluating the structural model (Hair et al. 2010). All measurement model parameters are for the model when using the full-information CFA approach (Anderson and Gerbing, 1982). granted that the normality of the data has been established. Maximum likelihood estimation techniques are used to estimate the parameters.

Each relationship between constructs and indicators that are represented in the Full Measurement Model is predetermined a priori from marketing theory, and the model consists of 20 latent variables and 91 indicators. Four latent variables are measured in the second order. Normative pressure and environmental orientation were measured through 9 and 13 items, respectively, whereas institutional pressure was measured using 6 items. Customer cooperation and reverse logistics were measured through 7 items each, while green purchases were measured through 8 items. Green marketing and organizational involvement were measured through four items each, green technology and green production through five items each, and green design and green distribution through three items each. Environmental Performance and Financial Performance was measured through 7 items each, Operational performance was measured through 5 items, and Social performance was measured through 6 items. Three constructs are permitted to co-vary with one another, and each indicator has

its unique error term (indicated by the curved covariance paths in the measurement model). One path from every latent variable to one of its indicators is fixed to have a value of 1.0 to determine the scale of each factor. The confirmatory factor model in this study is regarded as being identified using the three-indicator rule (Blunch 2008). Every factor in the model is required to have a minimum of three indications, according to the first criterion. Second, there must be no correlation between the error terms, and third, no manifest variable may be an indicator for more than one latent variable. The measurement model is not only identifiable, but it is also recursive.

4.2.3 Factor Loading

The measurement model was applied following the guidelines provided by the prior researcher. The initial model evaluation was based on the item's loading on the latent variables. Given the complexity of the proposed model, the standardized residual covariance matrix and the Modification indices were also assessed to pinpoint any problematic components. If the factor loading was less than 0.5, the item's standardized residual covariance absolute value was larger than 2.0 then the item was susceptible to removal. The model was run, and evaluated against this parameter, and the process was repeated. To meet these requirements, a total of 42 items were deleted.

4.2.4 Model Validity

As was already mentioned, all of the measurement model's constructs were present and were permitted to correlate with one another. Then came a confirmatory factor analysis. The degree to which the data and model fit one another was calculated using the AMOS software. While reliability refers to the accuracy of the concept scales, validity in surveys refers to the amount to which the survey measures the key things that need to be measured (i.e., its internal consistency). The ability of an instrument to measure what it is intended to measure is known as validity. Construct validity is further divided into the following classes and is a key component of the structural equation modeling process.

4.2.4.1 Content Validity

Content validity is a subjective assessment of "the relationship of the variables to be included in a summated scale and its conceptual meaning," in contrast to an empirical examination (Hair et al. 2010, p. 125). Two more areas of validity are crucial when assessing measurement models in SEM.

4.2.1.2 Convergent Validity

This concept sought to quantify the amount of an indication present in a single construct. An indicator is said to have converged if it has a high and significant factor loading value. Additionally, it has a standardized factor loading estimate that is greater than 0.5. Convergent validity is demonstrated when each factor is made up of variables that positively correlate with one another. Conversely, a construct demonstrates a high level of discriminant validity when it can be separated from the scales that make up the other variables in the model.

Convergent validity can be assessed by analyzing the factor loadings of the measurements on their respective constructs (Anderson &Gerbing, 1998). The authors suggest testing the statistical significance of the highest likelihood estimates first. These estimates represent unstandardized factor loadings between the constructs and their indicators, and they are known as regression weights in AMOS. Every unstandardized regression weight is statistically significant at the 5% level of significance.

The next step in determining convergent validity is to look at the standardized factor loadings of each indicator represented in the measurement model. Most experts agree that a minimal factor loading value of 0.50 is sufficient to show convergent validity, notwithstanding some academics' preference for a cut-off value of 0.70. (Hair et al. 2010).

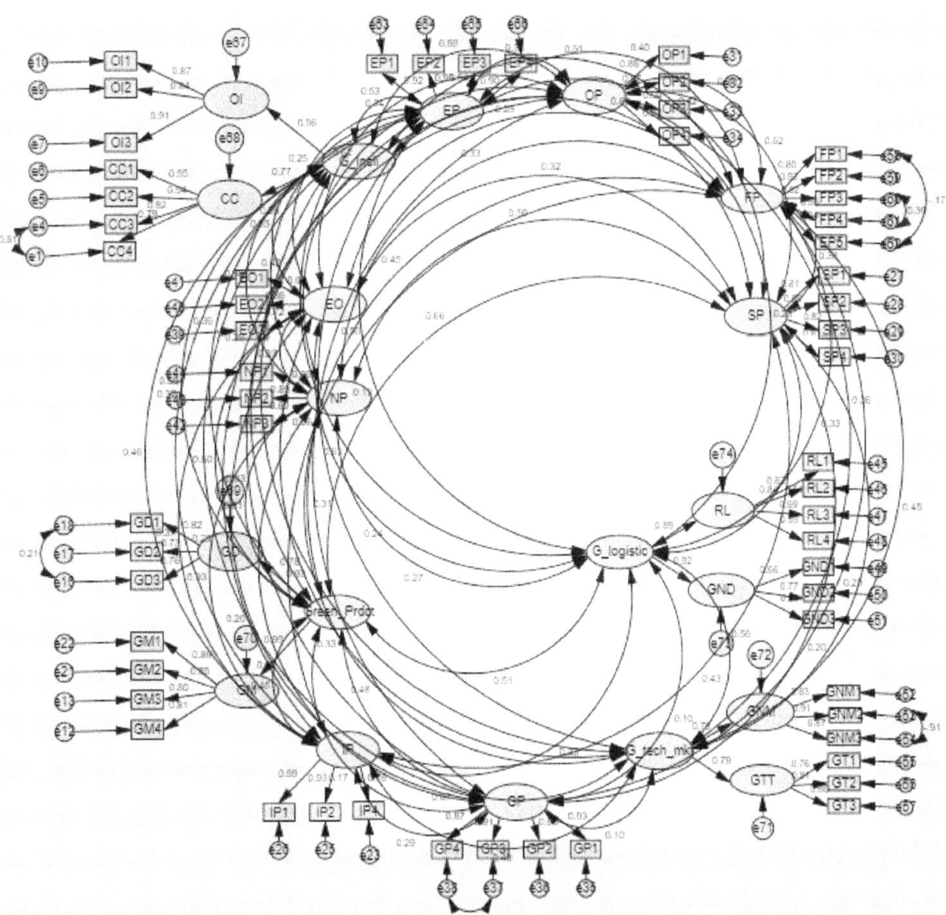

The tables below show the standardized factor loadings for each individual scale in the model:

Standardized Factor Loadings			
Indicator and latent variable			**Factor Loading**
OI	<---	G_Incli	0.955
CC	<---	G_Incli	0.770
GD	<---	Green_Prdct	0.926
GM	<---	Green_Prdct	0.995
RL	<---	G_logistic	0.890
GND	<---	G_logistic	0.921
GNM	<---	G_tech_mkt	0.782
GTT	<---	G_tech_mkt	0.792
CC4	<---	CC	0.792
CC3	<---	CC	0.822
CC2	<---	CC	0.942
CC1	<---	CC	0.948
GD3	<---	GD	0.760
GD2	<---	GD	0.734
GD1	<---	GD	0.818
IP4	<---	IP	0.759
IP2	<---	IP	0.927
IP1	<---	IP	0.992
SP1	<---	SP	0.810
SP2	<---	SP	0.883
SP3	<---	SP	0.820
SP4	<---	SP	0.811
OP1	<---	OP	0.859
OP2	<---	OP	0.870
OP3	<---	OP	0.943
OP4	<---	OP	0.933
GP1	<---	GP	0.934
GP2	<---	GP	0.946
GP3	<---	GP	0.808
GP4	<---	GP	0.865
EO3	<---	EO	0.721
EO2	<---	EO	0.862

EO1	<---	EO	0.647
NP3	<---	NP	0.894
NP2	<---	NP	0.894
NP1	<---	NP	0.856
RL1	<---	RL	0.820
RL2	<---	RL	0.843
RL3	<---	RL	0.693
RL4	<---	RL	0.832
GT1	<---	GTT	0.757
GT2	<---	GTT	0.806
GT3	<---	GTT	0.795
FP1	<---	FP	0.802
FP2	<---	FP	0.929
FP3	<---	FP	0.827
FP4	<---	FP	0.846
FP5	<---	FP	0.729
EP1	<---	EP	0.924
EP2	<---	EP	0.948
EP3	<---	EP	0.940
EP4	<---	EP	0.898
OI1	<---	OI	0.871
OI2	<---	OI	0.842
OI3	<---	OI	0.906
GM1	<---	GM	0.860
GM2	<---	GM	0.851
GM3	<---	GM	0.796
GM4	<---	GM	0.808
GND1	<---	GND	0.655
GND2	<---	GND	0.770
GND3	<---	GND	0.888
GNM1	<---	GNM	0.833
GNM2	<---	GNM	0.908
GNM3	<---	GNM	0.867

The factor loading for each scale is shown in the above table. They have a high degree of convergent validity and explain variance contributes to a bigger percentage of the measures' variance than error variance, as seen by the minimum factor loading of 0.647, which is higher than the tighter criteria of exceeding a minimum value of 0.50. (Hair et al. 2010). Even though factor loading provides a substantial amount of evidence in favor of convergent validity, AVE and CR are two further evaluations that are conducted to contribute to the body of knowledge.

Convergent validity can also be assessed using the average variance extracted (AVE) value of the construct. Hair et al. recommend that this value be greater than 0.5. (2000). AVE (Average Variance Extracted) is the abbreviation for the formula, and AVE values are:

$$\text{AVE} = \frac{\textit{Sum of Standardized Loadning Square}}{\textit{Sumof Standardized Loadning Square +measurement error}}$$

$$\text{Measurement error} = 1 - (\text{Stadardized Loading})^2$$

In addition to accounting for the construct's error variance, construct reliability (CR) assesses the same thing as the average variance extracted (AVE). The average amount of variation in a scale that can be explained by a latent variable is called the average variance extracted (AVE).

A good level of convergent validity can be seen by analyzing the AVE scores, which show that practically all loadings in all three models are larger than 0.50 and that each construct exceeded this threshold in at least one or more nation models.

Concept reliability (CR) is employed to evaluate the consistency of the construct validity indicator. The build dependability was calculated using the formula:

$$\text{CR} = \frac{\textit{Square of Total Standardized Loadning}}{\textit{Square of Total Standardized Loadning+measurement error}}$$

Average variance Extracted and construct Reliability		
	CR	**AVE**
Green Logistics	0.901	0.820
Institutional Pressure	0.925	0.806
Social Performance	0.900	0.691
Operational performance	0.946	0.814
Green Purchase	0.938	0.792
Environmental Orientation	0.790	0.560
Normative Pressure	0.913	0.777
Financial Performance	0.916	0.687
Environmental Performance	0.961	0.861
Green Inclination	0.857	0.752
Green Products	0.960	0.924
Green Techno Marketing	0.765	0.619

All constructs for the CR study exceeded the cut-off value of 0.70, showing strong support for convergent validity as well.

4.2.4.3 Discriminant Validity

Discriminant validity refers to how different a construct is from other constructions and how little it can be measured in the same way under a different notion. To demonstrate this form of validity, researchers usually compare the square root of the average variance extracted (AVE) from each construct with the estimated correlations between the constructs. If the square root AVE value of the variable is more than the anticipated correlation between it and another variable, there is evidence to suggest a suitable level of discriminant validity between these variables.

Discriminant Validity	Green Logistics	Institutional Pressure	Social Performance	Operational performance	Green Purchase	Environmental Orientation	Normative Pressure	Financial Performance	Environmental Performance	Green Inclination	Green Products	Green Techno Marketing
Green Logistics	**0.906**											
Institutional Pressure	0.331	**0.898**										
Social Performance	0.512	0.427	**0.832**									
Operational performance	0.228	0.285	0.618	**0.902**								
Green Purchase	0.101	0.289	0.203	0.059	**0.890**							
Environmental Orientation	0.238	0.372	0.323	0.338	0.198	**0.749**						
Normative Pressure	0.273	0.325	0.586	0.622	0.065	0.234	**0.882**					
Financial Performance	0.328	0.495	0.375	0.296	0.203	0.278	0.328	**0.829**				
Environmental Performance	0.134	0.318	0.421	0.308	0.027	0.251	0.265	0.395	**0.928**			
Green Inclination	0.628	0.457	0.826	0.586	0.227	0.328	0.584	0.513	0.528	**0.867**		
Green Products	0.505	0.447	0.657	0.415	0.168	0.504	0.509	0.440	0.364	0.694	**0.961**	
Green Techno Marketing	0.557	0.493	0.700	0.361	0.100	0.326	0.476	0.448	0.313	0.779	0.667	**0.787**

An overall finding shows these variables' discriminant validity when comparing square root AVE estimates to their matching correlation estimations. The discriminant validity test reveals the amount of variation present in the indicators that can be used to account for variation in the concept. Since AVE's square root is bigger than its correlation, the model's discriminant validity is strong.

As a result, additional evaluations show that the CFA model has adequate levels of reliability and validity, and performing route analyses using its approved constructs should result in statistically significant conclusions.

4.2.5 Goodness of Fit Analysis

The important measures of model fit are summarised in the table. According to Hair et al. (2010), three to four fit indices are sufficient to demonstrate model fit, and researchers should offer at least "one absolute fit index and one incremental fit index, in addition to the 2 findings." In addition, Kline (1998) recommends including a fit index that modifies the explained variance for the complexity of the model. The table includes a variety of fit statistics, including the chi-square statistic (χ2), the χ2/df (Normed χ2), the RMSEA (root mean square error of approximation), the incremental fit index (IFI), the Normed fit index (NFI), the comparative fit index (CFI), and the TLI (Tucker-Lewis index).

Model Fit Criteria						
Chi-square	CMIN/DF	RMSEA	NFI	CFI	TLI	IFI
3688.176	2.528	0.060	0.845	0.900	0.890	0.900

Hair et al. (2010) state that a model's degrees of freedom are computed as Df=1/2[(p)(p+1)]-k Where p is the number of observed variables and k is the number of estimated parameters.

4.2.5.1 Absolute Fit Indices

Absolute fit indices show which proposed model has the best fit and determine how well the a priori model matches the sample data (McDonald and Ho, 2002). The most basic indicator of how well the suggested hypothesis fits the data is provided by these metrics. Their methodology does not rely on comparison with a baseline model, unlike incremental fit indices; rather, it assesses how well the model fits in comparison to having no model at all (Jöreskog and Sörbom, 1993). The Chi-Squared test, RMSEA, RMSR, and SRMR fall under this group.

4.2.5.2 Model Chi-Square (χ2)

The standard metric for assessing overall model fit is the Chi-Square value, which "assesses the level of difference between the sample and fitted covariances matrices" (Hu and Bentler, 1999: 2). The Chi-Square statistic is frequently referred to as a "badness of fit" (Kline, 2005) or "lack of fit" (Mulaik et al, 1989) measure because a decent model fit would produce an insignificant result at a 0.05 threshold (Barrett, 2007).

Although the Chi-Squared test continues to be widely used as a fit statistic, there are many serious restrictions on its application. First off, even though the model is fully defined, this test presupposes multivariate normality and large departures from normality may lead to model rejections (McIntosh, 2006). The Chi-Square statistic is sensitive to sample size because it is essentially a statistical significance test, which means that it almost always rejects the model when large samples are utilized (Bentler and Bonnet, 1980; Jöreskog and Sörbom, 1993). On the other hand, the Chi-Square statistic lacks power when using small samples, making it potentially unable to distinguish between models with good and those with poor fit(Kenny and McCoach, 2003). Due to the Model Chi limitations, Square's researchers have looked for alternate metrics to judge model fit. The relative/normed chi- square ($\chi 2/df$) by Wheaton et al. (1977) is an illustration of a statistic that minimizes the effect of sample size on the Model Chi-Square. While recommendations range from as high as 5.0 (Wheaton et al., 1977) to as low as 2.0, there is no general agreement on what ratio is acceptable for this statistic (Tabachnick and Fidell, 2007). The ($\chi 2/df$) score for this model is 2.528, indicating a strong model fit.

3688.176 is the model's $\chi 2$ statistic as a whole. Concerning its $\chi 2$ value, it has a p-value of 0.000, demonstrating statistical significance at the 0.05 level. According to Kline (1998), large sample sizes have high power, which encourages the discovery of even the tiniest variations between the real model and the theoretical model, thus disproving the idea that there are no significant changes between the two models. To reach well-supported judgments on model fit, it is important to evaluate fit indices other than $\chi 2$.

4.2.5.3 Root Mean Square Error of Approximation (RMSEA)

Steiger and Lind invented the RMSEA first (1980, cited in Steiger, 1990). The RMSEA indicates how well the model would fit the population's covariance matrix if its parameter estimates were unknown but carefully chosen (Byrne, 1998). Due to its sensitivity to the number of estimated parameters in the model, it has recently come to be known as "one of the most informative fit indices" (Diamantopoulos and Siguaw, 2000: 85). To put it another way, the RMSEA favors parsimony by picking the model with the fewest parameters. In the past fifteen years, recommendations for RMSEA cut-off points have been significantly lowered.

Before the early 1990s, the reasonable fit was denoted by an RMSEA of 0.05 to 0.10, while the poor fit was denoted by values higher than 0.10. (MacCallum et al, 1996). Then, it was believed that an RMSEA of 0.08 to 0.10 offers a medium fit and that a value of less than 0.08 indicates an excellent fit (MacCallum et al, 1996). The table reveals the value of RMSEA which is 0.060 which indicates a good fit for the model.

4.2.5.4 Incremental Fit Indices

Incremental fit indices are a class of indices that do not use the chi-square in their raw form but instead compare the chi-square value to a baseline model (Miles and Shevlin, 2007; McDonald and Ho, 2002). The null hypothesis for these models is that all of the variables are uncorrelated (McDonald and Ho, 2002). The table reveals the value of Incremental Fit Indices which is 0.900 which indicates an excellent fit for the model.

4.2.5.5 Normed-Fit Index (NFI)

According to recent recommendations, the cut-off criteria should be NFI .80. (Hu and Bentler, 1999). This index has a significant flaw in that it is sensitive to sample size, underestimating fit for samples under 200 (Mulaik et al., 1989; Bentler, 1990), and should not be relied on exclusively as a result (Kline, 2005). The Tucker-Lewis index, also known as the Non-Normed Fit Measure (NNFI), a model preference index, was used to solve this issue. The table reveals the value of NFI as 0.845 which indicates an excellent fit for the model.

4.2.5.6 CFI (Comparative Fit Index)

Even with a small sample size, the Comparative Fit Index (CFI: Bentler, 1990), a modified version of the NFI that takes sample size into account, performs well (Byrne, 1998). 2007 (Tabachnick and Fidell). This index was first presented by Bentler (1990), and later on, it was one of the fit indices in his EQS program (Kline, 2005). To compare the sample covariance matrix with this null model, this statistic, like the NFI, makes the assumption that all latent variables are uncorrelated (null/independence model). Like the NFI, this statistic's values range from 0.0 to 1.0, with values closer to 1.0 indicating a strong fit. Initially, research pointed to a CFI 0.90 cutoff. The table reveals the value of CFI as 0.900 which indicates an excellent fit for the model.

4.2.5.7 TLI (Tucker-Lewis index)

An alternative method to measure incremental fit is the TLI statistic, often known as NNFI (the non- Normed fit index). The posited model is again compared to a null model or a nested baseline model. Other characteristics of the TLI measure that are analogous to the CFI include insensitivity to sample size variations and a usual range of values between zero and 1.0 (Marsh et al. 1998); however, TLI values are not constrained to this range and can go below zero and above 1.0. 2010; Hair et al. According to Bentler and Bonett (1988), a TLI score over a minimum cut-off of 0.90 indicates an acceptable level of model fit.

The TLI for the proposed model is 0.890, which indicates excellent model fit. As a result, the overall incremental fit indices support a strong model fit.

4.2.5.8 Structural Analysis

To test the study's hypotheses, a switch from a measurement model to a structural model is required.

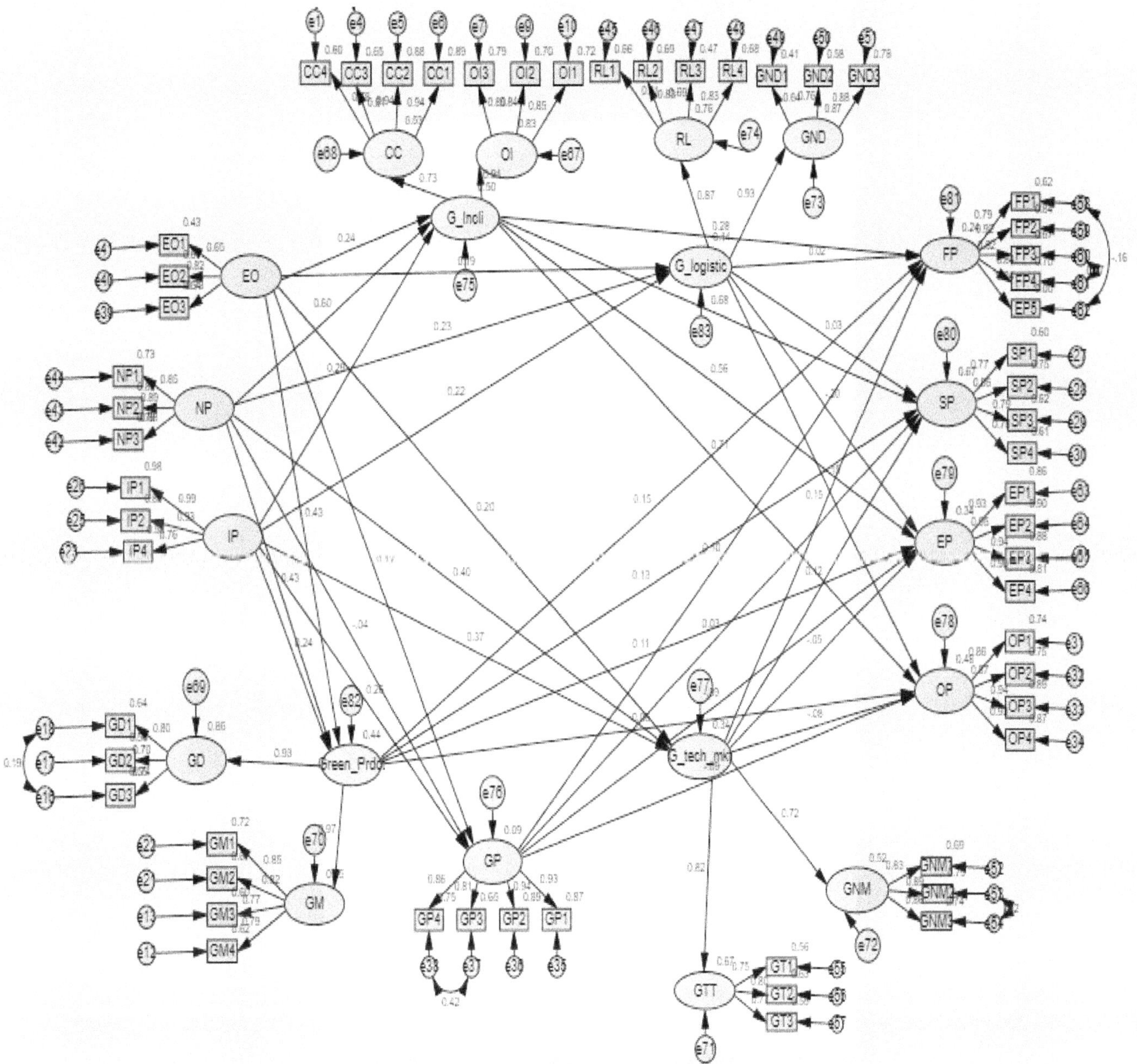

The CFA model's satisfactory goodness-of-fit metrics and the encouraging results of multiple construct reliability and validity tests support this choice. While some studies assess the structural model and measurement model simultaneously, the two-step SEM method developed by Anderson and Gerbing (1988) has some advantages. The researcher can first assess the measurement model's fit to a structural model with the poor match to address the GIGO (garbage in, garbage out) problem. In other words, the statistical outcomes of a structural model test with poor measures are useless. The two-step method also offers more statistics on model fit and validity than the one-step method, which only offers one important test of fit and validity (Hair et al. 2010, p. 711). In doing so, the researcher can determine whether the issues with her statistical analysis are the result of a poor hypothesis or insufficient measurements (Blunch 2008).

Path analysis (Regression weight)					
Dependent Variable		Independent Variable	**SRW**	**C.R.**	**P**
Green Inclination	<---	Environmental Orientation	0.239	4.808	***
Green Logistics	<---	Environmental Orientation	0.189	3.279	0.001
Green Techno Marketing	<---	Environmental Orientation	0.200	3.370	***
Green Purchase	<---	Environmental Orientation	0.123	2.297	0.022
Green Products	<---	Environmental Orientation	0.433	7.901	***
Green Inclination	<---	Normative Pressure	0.599	10.181	***
Green Logistics	<---	Normative Pressure	0.231	4.264	***
Green Techno Marketing	<---	Normative Pressure	0.401	6.646	***
Green Purchase	<---	Normative Pressure	-0.037	-0.734	0.463
Green Products	<---	Normative Pressure	0.435	8.940	***
Green Inclination	<---	Institutional Pressure	0.290	6.189	***
Green Logistics	<---	Institutional Pressure	0.219	4.145	***
Green Techno Marketing	<---	Institutional Pressure	0.372	6.297	***
Green Purchase	<---	Institutional Pressure	0.262	5.282	***
Green Products	<---	Institutional Pressure	0.242	5.394	***
Financial Performance	<---	Green Logistics	0.020	0.369	0.712
Social Performance	<---	Green Logistics	0.032	0.767	0.443
Environmental Performance	<---	Green Logistics	-0.205	-3.982	***
Operational performance	<---	Green Logistics	-0.151	-3.189	0.001
Financial Performance	<---	Green Inclination	0.279	4.357	***
Social Performance	<---	Green Inclination	0.681	9.687	***
Environmental Performance	<---	Green Inclination	0.562	8.281	***
Operational performance	<---	Green Inclination	0.712	9.750	***
Operational performance	<---	Green Techno Marketing	-0.075	-1.331	0.183
Environmental Performance	<---	Green Techno Marketing	-0.054	-0.894	0.371
Social Performance	<---	Green Techno Marketing	0.123	2.356	0.018
Financial Performance	<---	Green Techno Marketing	0.152	2.322	0.02
Financial Performance	<---	Green Purchase	0.103	2.169	0.03
Social Performance	<---	Green Purchase	0.026	0.693	0.489
Environmental Performance	<---	Green Purchase	-0.088	-1.994	0.046
Operational performance	<---	Green Purchase	-0.088	-2.137	0.033
Financial Performance	<---	Green Products	0.149	2.524	0.012
Social Performance	<---	Green Products	0.130	2.750	0.006
Environmental Performance	<---	Green Products	0.108	1.977	0.048
Operational performance	<---	Green Products	0.062	1.203	0.229

Various independent factors' effects on the dependent variables are depicted in the structural diagram.

Hypothesis-1:-

H_0: There is no significant impact of Environmental Orientation on green inclination

H_1: There is a significant impact of Environmental Orientation on green inclination

Interpretation:-

Environmental Orientation has a significant and positive impact on green inclination, according to the path diagram and table. *($\beta = 0.239$, $t = 4.808$, $p<0.0001$).*

Hypothesis-2:-

H_0: There is no significant impact of Environmental Orientation on Green Logistics

H_1: There is a significant impact of Environmental Orientation on Green Logistics

Interpretation:-

Environmental Orientation has a significant and positive impact on Green Logistics *($\beta = 0.189$, $t = 3.279$, $p=0.001$).*

Hypothesis-3:-

H_0: There is no significant impact of Environmental Orientation on green Techno Marketing

H_1: There is a significant impact of Environmental Orientation on green Techno Marketing

Interpretation:-

Environmental Orientation has a significant and positive impact on Green Techno Marketing *($\beta = 0.200$, $t = 3.370$, $p<0.0001$).*

Hypothesis-4:-

H_0: There is no significant impact of Environmental Orientation on green Purchase

H_1: There is a significant impact of Environmental Orientation on green Purchase

Interpretation:-

Environmental Orientation has a significant and positive impact on green purchase *($\beta = 0.123$, $t = 2.297$, $p=0.022$)* and green Products *($\beta = 0.433$, $t = 7.901$, $p<0.0001$).*

Hypothesis-5:-

H_0: There is no significant impact of normative pressure on green inclination

H_1: There is a significant impact of normative pressure on green inclination

Interpretation:-

Green Inclination is positively and significantly impacted by normative pressure (*β = 0.599, t = 10.181, p<0.0001*).

Hypothesis-6:-

H_0: There is no significant impact of normative pressure on green Logistics

H_1: There is a significant impact of normative pressure on green Logistics

Green Logistics is positively and significantly impacted by normative pressure (*β = 0.231, t = 4.2649, p<0.0001).*

Hypothesis-7:-

H_0: There is no significant impact of normative pressure on green Techno Marketing

H_1: There is a significant impact of normative pressure on green Techno Marketing

Green Techno Marketing is positively and significantly impacted by normative pressure (*β = 0.401, t = 6.646, p<0.0001).*

Hypothesis-8:-

H_0: There is no significant impact of normative pressure on green Product

H_1: There is a significant impact of normative pressure on green Product

Interpretation:-

Green Product is positively and significantly impacted by normative pressure (*β* = 0.435, t = 8.940, *p<0.0001).*

Hypothesis-9:-

H_0: There is no significant impact of normative pressure on green purchases

H_1: There is a significant impact of normative pressure on green purchases

Interpretation:-

Normative pressure affects green purchases negatively but not significantly (*β = -0.037, t = -0.734, p=0.463).*

Hypothesis-10:-

H_0: There is no significant impact of Institutional pressure on green inclination

H_1: There is a significant impact of Institutional pressure on green inclination

Interpretation:-

Green Inclination is positively and significantly impacted by institutional pressure (*β = 0.290, t = 6.189, p<0.0001*).

Hypothesis-11:-

H_0: There is no significant impact of institutional pressure on green Logistics

H_1: There is a significant impact of institutional pressure on green Logistics

Interpretation:-

Green Logistics is positively and significantly impacted by institutional pressure(*β = 0.219, t = 4.145, p<0.0001).*

Hypothesis- 12:-

H_0: There is no significant impact of institutional pressure on green Techno Marketing

H_1: There is a significant impact of institutional pressure on green Techno Marketing

Interpretation:-

Green Techno Marketing is positively and significantly impacted by institutional pressure (*β = 0.372, t = 6.297, p<0.0001).*

Hypothesis-13:-

H_0: There is no significant impact of institutional pressure on green Purchase

H_1: There is a significant impact of institutional pressure on green Purchase

Interpretation:-

Green Purchase is positively and significantly impacted by institutional pressure (*β = 0.262, t = 5.282, p<0.0001) and* Green Products (*β = 0.242, t = 5.394, p<0.0001).*

Hypothesis-14:-

H_0: There is no significant impact of green logistics on financial performance

H_1: There is a significant impact of green logistics on financial performance

Interpretation:-

The financial performance is positively but not significantly impacted by green logistics. (*β = 0.020, t = 4.357, p = 0.712)*

Hypothesis-15:-

H_0: There is no significant impact of green logistics on social performance

H_1: There is a significant impact of green logistics on social performance

Interpretation:-

Social performance is positively but not significantly impacted by green logistics. *(β = 0.032, t = 0.767, p = 0.443).*

Hypothesis-16:-

H_0: There is no significant impact of green logistics on environmental performance

H_1: There is a significant impact of green logistics on environmental performance

Interpretation:-

Green logistic has a negative and significant effect on environmental performance (*β* = -0.205, t = - *3.982, p<0.0001)*

Hypothesis-17:-

H_0: There is no significant impact of green logistics on Operational performance

H_1: There is a significant impact of green logistics on Operational performance

Interpretation:-

Green logistic has a negative and significant effect on Operational performance *(β = -0151, t = - 3.189, p = 0.001).*

Hypothesis-18:-

H_0: There is no significant impact of Green Inclination on financial performance

H_1: There is a significant impact of Green Inclination on financial performance

Green Inclination has a positive and significant effect on financial performance *(β = 0.279, t = 0.369, p<0.0001).*

Hypothesis-19:-

H_0: There is no significant impact of Green Inclination on social performance

H_1: There is a significant impact of Green Inclination on social performance

Interpretation:-

Green Inclination has a positive and significant effect on social performance *(β = 0.681, t = 9.687, p<0.0001).*

Hypothesis-20:-

H_0: There is no significant impact of Green Inclination on environmental performance

H_1: There is a significant impact of Green Inclination on environmental performance

Interpretation:-

Green Inclination has a positive and significant effect on environmental performance *($\beta = 0.562$, $t = 8.281$, $p<0.0001$)*

Hypothesis-21:-

H_0: There is no significant impact of Green Inclination on Operational performance

H_1: There is a significant impact of Green Inclination on Operational performance

Interpretation:-

Green Inclination has a positive and significant effect on Operational performance *($\beta = 0.712$, $t = 9.750$, $p<0.0001$).*

Hypothesis-22:-

H_0: There is no significant impact of Green Techno Marketing on Operational performance

H_1: There is a significant impact of Green Techno Marketing on Operational performance

Interpretation:-

Green Techno Marketing has a negative and non-significant effect on Operational performance *($\beta = -0.075$, $t = -1.331$, $p = 0.183$)*

Hypothesis-23:-

H_0: There is no significant impact of Green Techno Marketing on environmental performance

H_1: There is a significant impact of Green Techno Marketing on environmental performance

Interpretation:-

Green Techno Marketing has a negative and non-significant effect on environmental performance *($\beta = -0.054$, $t = -0.894$, $p = 0.371$).*

Hypothesis-24:-

H_0: There is no significant impact of Green Techno Marketing on social performance

H_1: There is a significant impact of Green Techno Marketing on social performance

Interpretation:-

Green Techno Marketing has a positive and significant effect on social performance (*β = 0.123, t = 2.365, p = 0.018)*

Hypothesis-25:-

H_0: There is no significant impact of Green Techno Marketing on financial performance

H_1: There is a significant impact of Green Techno Marketing on financial performance

Interpretation:-

Green Techno Marketing has a positive and significant effect on financial performance (*β = 0.152, t = 2.322, p = 0.0200).*

Hypothesis-26:-

H_0: There is no significant impact of **Green purchases** on social performance

H_1: There is a significant impact of Green purchases on social performance

Interpretation:-

The green purchase has a positive and non-significant effect on social performance (*β = 0.026, t = 0.693, p = 0.489).*

Hypothesis-27:-

H_0: There is no significant impact of Green purchase on financial performance

H_1: There is a significant impact of Green purchases on financial performance

Interpretation:-

The green purchase has a positive and significant effect on financial performance (*β = 0.103, t = 2.169, p = 0.0300).*

Hypothesis-28:-

H_0: There is no significant impact of Green purchases on environmental performance

H_1: There is a significant impact of Green purchases on environmental performance

Interpretation:-

The green purchase has a negative and significant effect on environmental performance (*β = -0.088, t = -1.994, p = 0.0460)*

Hypothesis-29:-

H_0: There is no significant impact of Green purchase on operational performance

H_1: There is a significant impact of Green purchase on operational performance

Interpretation:-

The green purchase has a negative and significant effect on operational performance (*β = -0.088, t = -2.137, p = 0.033*).

Hypothesis-30:-

H_0: There is no significant impact of Green products on financial performance

H_1: There is a significant impact of Green products on financial performance

Interpretation:-

Green product has a positive and significant effect on financial performance (*β = 0.149, t = 2.524, p = 0.012*).

Hypothesis-31:-

H_0: There is no significant impact of Green products on social performance

H_1: There is a significant impact of Green products on social performance

Interpretation:-

Green product has a positive and significant effect on social performance (*β = 0.130, t = 2.750, p = 0.006*)

Hypothesis-32:-

H_0: There is no significant impact of Green products on environmental performance

H_1: There is a significant impact of Green products on environmental performance

Interpretation:-

Green product has a positive and significant effect on environmental performance (*β = 0.108, t = 1.977, p = 0.048*).

Hypothesis- 33:-

H_0: There is no significant impact of Green products on Operational performance

H_1: There is a significant impact of Green products on Operational performance

Interpretation:-

Green product has a positive and non-significant effect on Operational performance (*β = 0.062, t = 1.203, p = 0.229*).

4.2.5 Hypothesis Testing Summary

Sr. No	Hypothesis	Significance Value (P value)	Result
1	H_0: There is no significant impact of Environmental Orientation on green inclination	*p<0.001*	Rejected
2	H_0: There is no significant impact of Environmental Orientation on Green Logistics	*p=0.001*	Rejected
3	H_0: There is no significant impact of Environmental Orientation on green Techno Marketing	*p<0.001*	Rejected
4	H_0: There is no significant impact of Environmental Orientation on green Purchase	*p<0.001*	Rejected
5	H_0: There is no significant impact of normative pressure on green inclination	*p<0.001*	Rejected
6	H_0: There is no significant impact of normative pressure on green Logistics	*p<0.001*	Rejected
7	H_0: There is no significant impact of normative pressure on green Techno Marketing	*p<0.001*	Rejected
8	H_0: There is no significant impact of normative pressure on green Product	*p<0.001*	Rejected
9	H_0: There is no significant impact of normative pressure on green purchases	*p=0.463*	Fail to Reject Null Hypothesis
10	H_0: There is no significant impact of institutional pressure on green inclination	*p<0.001*	Rejected
11	H_0: There is no significant impact of institutional pressure on green Logistics	*p<0.001*	Rejected
12	H_0: There is no significant impact of institutional pressure on green Techno Marketing	*p<0.001*	Rejected
13	H_0: There is no significant impact of institutional pressure on green Purchase	*p<0.001*	Rejected
14	H_0: There is no significant impact of green logistics on financial performance	*p = 0.712*	Fail to Reject Null Hypothesis
15	H_0: There is no significant impact of green logistics on social performance	*p = 0.443*	Fail to Reject Null Hypothesis
16	H_0: There is no significant impact of green logistics on environmental performance	*p<0.001*	Rejected
17	H_0: There is no significant impact of green logistics on Operational performance	*p = 0.001*	Rejected
18	H_0: There is no significant impact of Green Inclination on financial performance	*p<0.001*	Rejected

19	H_0: There is no significant impact of Green Inclination on social performance	$p<0.001$	Rejected
20	H_0: There is no significant impact of Green Inclination on environmental performance	$p<0.001$	Rejected
21	H_0: There is no significant impact of Green Inclination on Operational performance	$p<0.001$	Rejected
22	H_0: There is no significant impact of Green Techno Marketing on Operational performance	$p = 0.183$	Fail to Reject Null Hypothesis
23	H_0: There is no significant impact of Green Techno Marketing on environmental performance	$p = 0.371$	Fail to Reject Null Hypothesis
24	H_0: There is no significant impact of Green Techno Marketing on social performance	$p = 0.018$	Rejected
25	H_0: There is no significant impact of Green Techno Marketing on financial performance	$p = 0.0200$	Rejected
26	H_0: There is no significant impact of Green purchases on social performance	$p = 0.489$	Fail to Reject Null Hypothesis
27	H_0: There is no significant impact of Green purchase on financial performance	$p = 0.0300$	Rejected
28	There is no significant impact of Green purchases on environmental performance	$p = 0.0460$	Rejected
29	H_0: There is no significant impact of Green purchase on operational performance	$p = 0.033$	Rejected
30	H_0: There is no significant impact of Green products on financial performance	$p = 0.012$	Rejected
31	H_0: There is no significant impact of Green products on social performance	$p = 0.006$	Rejected
32	H_0: There is no significant impact of Green products on environmental performance	$p = 0.048$	Rejected
33	H_0: There is no significant impact of Green products on operational performance	$p = 0.229$	Rejected

Summary:

To Summarize data analysis, this chapter has discussed the data analysis as well as the results in detail. The researcher has applied confirmatory factor analysis, path analysis and validated the research model, and tested the hypothesis.

Initially, the researcher applied Cronbach's alpha value and found that construct alpha values exceeded the standard values as Cronbach's alpha value was 0.955 which was more than the minimum benchmark value of 0.7 which indicates that the data is reliable for further study.

The researcher found that all 424 respondents are aware of the concept of Green Supply Chain Management. The researcher concludes that around 78.8% of manufacturing firms are in the emergence or Initial stage of the green supply chain. The lowest factor loading is 0.647 which is above the benchmark value of 0.5 which demonstrates a high level of convergent validity.

The researcher has found a high level of discriminant validity as AVE's square root is bigger than its correlation. Further analysis concludes that the CFA model has adequate levels of reliability and validity, and performing route analyses using its approved constructs should result in statistically significant conclusions.

All Incremental fit indices ranging from NFI, CFI, IFI, and TLI values are above 0.7 which indicates a strong model fit. The structural diagram shows the effect of various independent variables on the dependent variables.

The researcher has measured the effect of Environmental Orientation, Normative Pressure, and Institutional Pressure on Green Inclination, Green Logistics, Green Techno Marketing, Green Purchases and Green Products. The researcher has also measured the effect of Green logistics, Green Inclination, Green techno marketing, Green Purchases and Green Products on Environmental, Operational, Social, and Financial Performance.

Next chapter focuses on the findings, Managerial Implications, and Conclusion of the study.

CHAPTER-5

Findings and Implications

5.1 Findings of the Study

1. It was found that the mean of 7 initial statements of the GSCM Awareness variable was found to be more than 3 indicating respondents' agreement with the statements. None of the statements was found to have a mean less than 3. Hence bringing social awareness about initiatives taken for the welfare of society, the advancement in technology, and the rising new business opportunities are key points of awareness.
2. From the frequency distribution, it was discovered that most of the frequencies are for strong agreement which establishes that the estimated advantage and consciousness of GSCM practices, rising in new business opportunities, enhancement of existing and new employees in the organization, Advancement in technology, initiatives are made towards rectification of issues related to the implementation of Green practices, attention for the promotion of Internet

   + Green manufacturing encourages to adopt GSCM and social awareness or publicizing about the initiative of a company doing a favor to society are the variables where the respondents' response is extensively towards the agreement that awareness is being prevailed highly by considering these factors. Consequently, it is established that there is awareness of Green Supply Chain Management in the companies of Gujarat.
3. It was found that the mean of 6 initial statements of the Institutional Pressure variable was found to be more than 3 indicating respondents' agreement with the statements. None of the statements was found to have a mean less than 3. It can be analyzed that factors such as safety assurance, constant audits, and regular government examination are the leading factors for Intuitional pressure
4. It was found that the mean of 13 initial statements of the Normative Pressure variable was found to be more than 3 indicating respondents' agreement with the statements. None of the statements was found to have a mean less than 3. Considering the mean value, it was found factors such as cooperation of the customer for a clean environment, the demand of

customers for the eco-design products, customers' preference for green products encourages, the upward set-up of supply chain supplier to manufacture, market demand, awareness about the eco-design of the product and audit of the supplier are leading factors for Normative Pressure.

5. It was found that the mean of 9 initial statements of the Environmental Orientation variable was found to be more than 3 indicating respondents' agreement with the statements. None of the statements was found to have a mean less than 3. Consequently, factors such as the policy of designing products in recyclable form, top-level management dedication towards the application of green supply chain management, the continuous support of senior managers and top-level management, and corporate value of the organization to safeguard the environment are the major factors for Environment Orientation. Therefore, from the analysis it was established that these drivers are playing a pivotal role in the adoption of GSCM Practices.
6. It was established that manufacturing companies of Gujarat are majorly following external practices such as Green Purchase, Customer Cooperation, and Reverse Logistics as the mean of most of the statements of this variable is more than 3. Thereupon, it was discovered that the companies of Gujarat follow these External Green Practices as a part of GSCM.
7. Based on analysis, it was learned that internal practices such as Green Design, Green Manufacturing, Green Marketing, Green Distribution, and Organizational Involvement are the practices that are followed by the manufacturing companies of Gujarat. As the mean of the statements of these variables is more than 3. Thus, it was observed that the above-mentioned Internal Green Practices are being extensively followed by the companies of Gujarat.
8. For Organizational Performance based on the data analysis, it was identified that Financial Performance, Environmental Performance, Operational Performance, and Social Performance are highly positively impacted by the application of the GSCM Practices. Since the mean of statements of these performances were found to be more than 3 indicating respondents' agreement for the statements. None of the statements was found to have a mean of less than 3. On that account, it was evaluated that the adoption of Green Practices is leading to boosting the Performance of the manufacturing Companies of Gujarat.
9. In every instance, it was found that the construct alpha values exceeded the standard values. It was found that the alpha values were 0.955. Therefore, it was found that the data is reliable for further study.
10. The minimum factor loading is 0.647, exceeding the stricter test of exceeding a minimum value of 0.50, indicating that they have a high degree of convergent validity and that explain variance contributes to a greater proportion of the variance in the measures than error variance. All constructs for the CR study went beyond the threshold of 0.70, showing strong support for convergent validity as well. The discriminant validity test reveals the amount of

variation present in the indicators that can be used to account for variation in the concept. Since AVE's square root is bigger than its correlation, the model's discriminant validity is strong. As a result, additional evaluations show that the CFA model has adequate levels of reliability and validity, and performing route analyses using its approved constructs should result in statistically significant conclusions.

11. The ($\chi2$/df) score for the CFA model is 2.528, indicating a strong model fit.3688.176 is the model's $\chi2$ statistic as a whole. Regarding its $\chi2$ value, it has a p-value of 0.000, demonstrating statistical significance at the 0.05 level. It is typically provided along with RMSEA, and in a well-fitting model, the top limit should be less than 0.08 and the lower limit should be near to 0. The value of RMSEA which is 0.060 that indicates a good fit for the model. The incremental fit indices (NFI, CFI, IFI, and TLI) for the proposed model are 0.845, 0.900, and 0.890, which are virtually at the acceptable level of 0.9. As a result, the overall incremental fit indices support a strong model fit.
12. The structural diagram shows the effect of various independent variables on the dependent variables. Path diagram and table indicate that Environmental Orientation has the positive and significant effect on Green Inclination *(β = 0.239, t = 4.808, p<0.0001)*, Green Logistics *(β = 0.189, t = 3.279, p=0.001)*, Green Techno Marketing *(β = 0.200, t = 3.370, p<0.0001)*, Green Purchase *(β = 0.123, t = 2.297, p=0.022) and* Green Products *(β = 0.433, t = 7.901, p<0.0001).*
13. Normative pressure has a positive and significant impact on Green Inclination *(β = 0.599, t= 10.181, p<0.0001)*, Green Logistics *(β = 0.231, t = 4.2649, p<0.0001)*, Green Techno Marketing *(β = 0.401, t = 6.646, p<0.0001)* and Green Product *(β = 0.435, t = 8.940, p<0.0001).* Where Normative pressure has a negative but non-significant impact on Green Purchase *(β = -0.037, t = -0.734, p=0.463).*
14. Institutional Pressure has a positive and significant effect on Green Inclination *(β = 0.290, t= 6.189, p<0.0001*), Green Logistics *(β = 0.219, t = 4.145, p<0.0001)*, Green Techno Marketing *(β = 0.372, t = 6.297, p<0.0001)*, Green Purchase *(β = 0.262, t = 5.282, p<0.0001) and* Green Products *(β = 0.242, t = 5.394, p<0.0001).*
15. Green logistic has a positive and non-significant effect on the financial performance *(β = 0.020, t = 4.357, p = 712)* and social performance *(β = 0.032, t = 0.767, p = 0.443).* Where Green logistics has a negative and significant effect on environmental performance *(β = - 0.205, t = -3.982, p<0.0001)* and Operational performance *(β = -0151, t = -3.189, p = 0.001).*
16. Green Inclination has a positive and significant effect on financial performance *(β = 0.279, t= 0.369, p<0.0001)*, social performance *(β = 0.681, t = 9.687, p<0.0001)*, environmental performance *(β = 0.562, t = 8.281, p<0.0001)* and Operational performance *(β = 0.712, t = 9.750, p<0.0001).*
17. Green Techno Marketing has a negative and non-significant effect on Operational performance *(β = -0.075, t = -1.331, p = 0.183)* and environmental performance *(β = -0.054, t = -0.894, p = 0.371).*

Where Green Techno Marketing has a positive and significant effect on social performance *(β = 0.123, t = 2.365, p = 0.018)* and financial performance *(β = 0.152, t = 2.322, p = 0.0200).*

18. Green purchase has a positive and non-significant effect on social performance *(β = 0.026, t = 0.693, p = 0.489),* Where Green purchase has a positive and significant effect on financial performance *(β = 0.103, t = 2.169, p = 0.0300).* Where Green purchase has a negative and significant effect on the environmental performance *(β = -0.088, t = -1.994, p = 0.0460)* and operational performance *(β = -0.088, t = -2.137, p = 0.033).*
19. Green product has a positive and significant effect on financial performance *(β = 0.149, t = 2.524, p = 0.012),* social performance *(β = 0.130, t = 2.750, p = 0.006),* and environmental performance *(β = 0.108, t = 1.977, p = 0.048).* Where a Green product has a positive and non-significant effect on the Operational performance *(β = 0.062, t = 1.203, p = 0.229).*
20. The incremental fit indices (NFI, CFI, IFI, and TLI) for the proposed model are 0.845, 0.900, and 0.890, which are virtually at the acceptable level of 0.80. As a result, the overall incremental fit indices support a strong model fit.

5.2 Managerial Implications

The empirical outcomes attained the objectives of the research and created ample evidence for the practitioners that practices like Green Inclination, Green Logistics, Green Techno marketing, Green Purchase and Green Products are having an impact on the overall performance of the companies. This can be used as a guide to the managers to understand the significance of the different green practices and to what extent these practices can play a vital role in enhancing the performance dimensions of the manufacturing companies.

In the context of Gujarat, this research gave rise to the distinct result that Institutional pressure is the significant pressure for the manufacturing industries the adoption of Sustainability Practices. Institutional pressure is having a positive impact on the Green Supply Chain Management Practices stipulates an evident linkage between the organizations and governments legislation also with the prevailing competition in the market. Therefore, regular audits, coordination, and cooperation with the government can boost the implementation of the GMSC. Apart from this, the present research study can be useful to the government (policymaker) for recognizing the importance of imposing taxes, and duties and enforcing the law for the proper implementation of GSCM and the protection of the environment.

Environmental orientation also plays a significant role in the adoption the green practices. From the present research, it was found that it has a positive and significant effect which drives the manufacturing companies for integration of the Green Practices in the process of Supply Chain. Safeguarding the environment by the manufacturing companies should be considered on the priority list which leads to the enhancement of the corporate value of the organization. Hence this study can be considered a source of encouragement as it provides evidence of growth in the corporate value by adopting the GSCM practices. Also, continuous support of the senior managers and proper teamwork can result in the successful implementation of the GSCM. Policies of the manufacturing companies considering the recyclable design of a product in the manufacturing process can also succor in following the GSCM. Framing the organization's environmental standards and allocating responsibility to a specific department that keeps a close check can pursue companies on the following of best green practices.

Normative pressure as well as a significant role in implementation the of green practices. As it takes into consideration the collaboration with stakeholders, suppliers, and customers. This study provides a strong base for developing an eminent strategy which can strengthen the relationship with these external parties and thereby companies can set out to determine if implementing GSCM methods that are centered on working with suppliers and customers can enhance environmental performance and, as a result, enhance organizational performance. The normative pressure can also be fruit- bearing to the regulators or policymakers and the companies for proactive commitment to embracing the GSCM.

Again, it was found that the manufacturing companies of Gujarat follow the approach which is reactive as per the provided evidence from the study under the pressure of Normative and Institutional. Specific practices are being followed concerning certain practices just to evade the fines, penalties, and dropping of market share.

The theorized and empirically supported model provides a structured method for successfully implementing an environmental sustainability strategy that necessitates direct collaboration between manufacturers and suppliers as well as customers to achieve the desired outcomes—an improved environment with a corresponding improvement in firm performance. Before putting green practices into place, it is crucial to adopt environmental sustainability as a strategic objective and alter current enterprise information systems to track the processes and results connected to the organization's sustainability initiatives. Manufacturers can start implementing sustainability practices with some assurance that the practices will lead to improved operational and organizational performance in addition to improved environmental and economic performance once environmental sustainability has been made a strategic focus and information systems have been modified to monitor efforts to become environmentally sustainable. The organization's ability to preserve the environment and increase its financial sustainability are both enhanced by the implementation of GSCM principles.

Major corporations have started putting in place comprehensive procedures to regulate environmental behavior across their supplier chains (Vachon, 2007). Collaboration, monitoring, and management of the environment are specifically supported by the following activities; monitoring reverse material flows; exchanging environmental management methods and knowledge with supply chain partners; working to reduce the environmental risk connected to suppliers' operations; and striving to ensure proper product use (Vachon, 2007).

"In the end, such activities with suppliers or with consumers might affect environmental management decisions within any individual manufacturing plant," claims Vachon (2007, p. 4357). The GSCM practices scales created by Zhu et al. (2008a) include items that outline the qualities of manufacturers who engage in environmental collaboration and monitoring with suppliers and clients. These traits give manufacturers who want to integrate environmental policies throughout their supply chains more precise guidance.

In addition, it was accomplished from the study that Green Inclination and Green Products have a remarkable impact on the comprehensive enrichment of performance. Green inclination which is weighing importance to factors like customer orientation and organizational improvement gives a proper justification that both are the dominant and key variables in fruitful implementation of clean practices. Thus, cross-sectional cooperation, interaction, and dissemination of information among the employees of several departments, efforts of the organization for proper linkage establishment between the environmental objectives with the corporate goals, and strong commitment from the top management are essentials for the adoption of GSCM. Besides this, the managers show also focus on providing training and development of the effective implementation of GSCM which requires upgraded skill and knowledge concerning the factors of sustainability and environmentalism. Moreover, according to the findings, the practice of Green Products which involves green manufacturing and green design as a chief factor is having a positive impact on all the criteria of performance. Therefore, this research can be fruitful to the organization in inculcating standard and recyclable eco-friendly design in the products and processes of production. Thereupon these manufacturing industries can focus on the minimization of toxic and hazardous waste and optimization of consumption of material and energy.

Furthermore, this research brings to the notice that in the current scenario, the market is customer-centric. So, the review of customers, preference of customers, and collaboration with customers for inculcating eco design in the process, for cleaner production, and green purchasing plays an ingenious role in applying the GSCM in companies. This point can be acknowledged by the companies in increasing their performance.

As per this research also Green Practices such as green logistics, Green purchase, and Green techno marketing have a noteworthy hand in embracing financial, social, operational, and environmental performance. So, the manufacturers can target these practices too in the correct acquisition of GSCM.

The findings of the study will be beneficial to both environmental enthusiasts as well as manufacturers to decide whether or not to engage in green supply chain management practices. As a part of CSR, the companies and brands will be able to use this study to gain an added advantage by considering green supply chain management as a CSR activity.

Industry leaders can assess the effects of various enhancements and modifications about the context of GSCM procedures using the factors derived from this study. Consequently, this research can be used as a flourishing origin which can be a tool for motivation, strategy formation, enabling proper training, and providing insightful knowledge to the associate parties for proper application of clean practices.

CHAPTER-6

Conclusion, Further Scope of Study, and Limitations

6.1 Conclusion

First and foremost, it can be elucidated that present research has expanded recent knowledge on the theoretical aspects fostering the impact of separate institutional and environmental orientation as a pressure on GSCM practices. Secondly, this study has played a key role in displaying the role of various theories in recognizing the complicated character of GSCM merely by encompassing path dependency theory which helps in providing fruitful insights to the companies in taking the right decision of adopting the GSCM practices can positively have a booming consequent impact on the economic, social, operational and environmental performance. Thirdly this research is gainful as it has eminently observed the Institutional pressure, Environmental orientation, and Normative pressure along with GSCM practices and also considered the financial, social, operational, and environmental performance in a dynamic single model for the manufacturing companies of Gujarat. Moreover, this research has been conducive in extensively considering the recommendations in two ways a) by empirically validating the study taking into consideration the previous scholars' work as a base while characterizing new few feasible elements for the various pressure-practices and performance direction. Furthermore, this study has explored a new model considering the major practices of GSCM and successfully examining their impact on different organizations' performances. Finally, this research has broadened the evolving mode of investigations in GSCM consciousness and application at a top-level consideration instead of unit level: doubtlessly such top- drawn construct and their correlation can augment the directional decision-making proficiency, competency, and their results.

6.2 Scope for Further Studies

The entire theoretical model is being tested with limited samples, so it's critical to evaluate the model using information from additional samples. Differences were found when comparing the findings to those published by Zhu and Sarkis (2007) concerning the influence of customer collaboration and investment recovery on environmental and economic performance. The discrepancies could be attributed to the different samples used in the two studies, one by Zhu and Sarkis (2007) using Chinese manufacturers and the other by this study's US producers. To resolve these discrepancies, more study is required. Verification of the results with a bigger sample is also crucial. This study can be extended to other states to observe the present GSCM scenario in India in broader aspects. This research also emphasizes how manufacturing organizations use Green Supply chain Management methods. Data should be gathered to examine the influence of supply chain methods on the organizational performance of these various types of companies, and the model should be changed to accommodate more organization types, such as wholesalers and retailers.

The researcher has created a Green Supply Chain Management model that focuses on the performance effects of GSCM methods used by manufacturing businesses to integrate and coordinate environmental sustainability activities with their supply chain partners. While analyzing each of the associations represented in the model individually is important, what matters most is how effectively the model as a whole represents reality. The model-level results imply that the supply chain and the operational business processes that extend throughout the supply chain should be considered when implementing Green Supply chain Management procedures. It is crucial to evaluate constructs reflecting different improvement programs, such as JIT, TQM, lean manufacturing, and agile manufacturing as potential antecedents to GSCM techniques while keeping in mind the contextual approach. Further, a study can be done across different states, with different demographics, or with a higher sample size for the unique findings.

6.3 Limitations

1. The present study has samples from Gujarat State only that is not representing the entire population of India.
2. The lack of response from some of the manufacturing firms who have adopted green supply chains posed as an obstruction.
3. The sample size for the current study is restricted, which also turned out to be a barrier.
4. Further study can be done as a comparative analysis across various states, which has not been done in the present study.
5. Moreover, limitations of fieldwork and research process applies to the current study as well.

CHAPTER-7

Bibliography

1. Abdullah, M. Hassan, and N. Johari, "Exploring the Linkage of Supply Chain Integration between Green Supply Chain Practices and Sustainable Performance: a Conceptual Link". In 4th International Conference on Future Environment and Energy, pp. 116-120, 2014.

2. Acharya, A., & Gupta, M. (2016). An application of brand personality to green consumers: A thematic analysis. The Qualitative Report, 21(8), 1531-1545. Retrieved from https://www.proquest.com/scholarly-journals/application-brand-personality-green- consumers/docview/2218839306/se-2

3. Acquaye, A., Genovese, A., Barrett, J., & Lenny Koh, S. C. (2014). Benchmarking carbon emissions performance in supply chains. Supply Chain Management, 19(3), 306-321. doi:https://doi.org/10.1108/SCM-11-2013-0419

4. Agyabeng-Mensah, Y., Ahenkorah, E., Afum, E., Adu, N. A., Agnikpe, C., & Rogers, F. (2020). Examining the influence of internal green supply chain practices, green human resource management and supply chain environmental cooperation on firm performance. Supply Chain Management, 25(5), 585-599. doi:https://doi.org/10.1108/SCM- 11-2019-0405

5. Ahmed, M. U., Kristal, M. M., Pagell, M., & Gattiker, T. F. (2017). Towards a classification of supply chain relationships: A routine based perspective. Supply Chain Management, 22(4), 341-374. doi:https://doi.org/10.1108/SCM-04-2017-0142

6. Akkermans, H. A., & Van Wassenhove, L.,N. (2018). A dynamic model of managerial response to grey swan events in supply networks. International Journal of Production Research, 56(1-2), 10-21. doi:https://doi.org/10.1080/00207543.2017.1395492

7. Alexander, A., Walker, H., & Naim, M. (2014). Decision theory in sustainable supply chain management: a literature review. Supply Chain Management: An International Journal.

8. Al-Hakimi, M., & Borade, D. B. (2020). The impact of entrepreneurial orientation on the supply chain resilience. Cogent Business & Management, 7(1) doi:https://doi.org/10.1080/23311975.2020.1847990

9. Alora, A., & Barua, M. K. (2021). The effect of supply chain disruptions on shareholder wealth in small and mid-cap companies. Supply Chain Management: An International Journal, 26(2), 212-223.

10. Al-Shboul, M. (2017). Infrastructure framework and manufacturing supply chain agility: The role of delivery dependability and time to market. Supply Chain Management, 22(2), 172-185. doi:https://doi.org/10.1108/SCM-09-2016-0335

11. Amin, M., & Khan, F. (2021). Green products: An overview. In M. A. Qureshi, A. G. Rana, & S. S. Hasan (Eds.), Handbook of Sustainable Development Goals and Indicators (pp. 107- 121). Springer.

12. Angell, L.C. and Klassen, R.D. (1999), "Integrating environmental issues into the mainstream: an agenda for research in operations management", Journal of Operations Management, Vol. 17 No. 5, pp. 575-98.

13. Arora, S., & Cason, T. N. (1996). Why do firms volunteer to exceed environmental regulations? Understanding participation in EPA's 33/50 program. Land Economics, 72(4), 413-432.

14. Asch, S. E. (1951). Effects of group pressure upon the modification and distortion of judgments. Groups, leadership and men, 222-236.

15. Ashayeri, J., Heuts, R. and Jansen, A. (1996). Inventory management of repairable service parts for personal computers. International Journal of Operational and Production Management, 16, 74 – 97.

16. Ashby, A., Leat, M., & Hudson-Smith, M. (2012). Making connections: a review of supply chain management and sustainability literature. Supply chain management: an international journal, 17(5), 497-516.

17. Bamberg, S., & Möser, G. (2007). Twenty years after Hines, Hungerford, and Tomera: A new meta-analysis of psycho-social determinants of pro-environmental behavior. Journal of Environmental Psychology, 27(1), 14-25.

18. Barros, A.I., Dekker, R. and Scholten, V. (1998). A two-level network for recycling sand: a case study. European Journal of Operational Research, 110, 199–214.

19. Biege, S., Felmeden, J., & Hertenstein, P. (2021). Green products: Definition and characteristics. In J. Barkemeyer, J. Preuss, & S. Lee (Eds.), The Oxford Handbook of the Responsible Management of Consumption (pp. 115-130). Oxford University Press.

20. Bouzon, M.; Govindan, K.; Rodriguez, C.M.T. Evaluating barriers for reverse logistics implementation under a multiple stakeholders' perspective analysis using grey decision making approach. Resour. Conserv. Recycle. 2018, 128, 315–335.

21. Bowen, F. E., Cousins, P. D., Lamming, R. C., & Faruk, A. C. (2001). The role of supply management capabilities in green supply. Production and Operations Management, 10(2), 174-189. Retrieved from https://www.proquest.com/scholarly-journals/role-supply- management-capabilities-green/docview/228741538/se-2

22. Carter, C. R., & Rogers, D. S. (2008). A framework of sustainable supply chain management: Moving toward new theory. International Journal of Physical Distribution & Logistics Management, 38(5), 360-387.

23. Centobelli, P.; Cerchione, R.; Esposito, E. Environmental sustainability and energy-efficient supply chain management: A review of research trends and proposed guidelines. Energies 2018, 11, 275.

24. Chandak, A., Kumar, N., & Dalpati, A. (2019). The Relationship Between Supply Chain Strategy and Supply Chain Performance: An Empirical Investigation Using Structural Equation Modeling. IUP Journal of Supply Chain Management, 16(4).

25. Chandra Shukla, A.; Deshmukh, S.; Kanda, A. Environmentally responsive supply chains: Learnings from the Indian auto sector. J. Adv. Manag. Res. 2009, 6, 154–171.

26. Chen, H., Geng, Y., Fujita, T., & Zhu, Q. (2014). A review of energy and environmental policy in China: The trend for green supply chain. Journal of Cleaner Production, 63, 143-168.

27. Chen, Y. (2008), "The driver of green innovation and green image – green core competence", Journal of Business Ethics, Vol. 81 No. 3, pp. 531-543

28. Chien, M.K. and Shih, L.H. (2007), "An empirical study of the implementation of green supply chain management practices in the electrical and electronic industry and their relation to organizational performances", Int. J. Environ. Sci. Tech, Vol. 4 No. 3, pp. 383-394

29. Chun, S. H., Hwang, H. J., & Byun, Y. H. (2015). Supply chain process and green business activities: Application to small and medium enterprises. Procedia-Social and Behavioral Sciences, 186, 862-867.

30. Cialdini, R. B., & Goldstein, N. J. (2004). Social influence: Compliance and conformity. Annual Review of Psychology, 55, 591-621

31. De Groot, J. I. M., & Steg, L. (2018). Educational interventions promoting pro-environmental attitudes and behaviours: A meta-analysis. Journal of Environmental Psychology, 59, 77-95. doi: 10.1016/j.jenvp.2018.09.003

32. Delmas, M., Toffel, M.W., 2004. Stakeholders and environmental management practices: an institutional framework. Business Strategy and the Environment 13, 209e222.

33. Diabat, A. and Govindan, K. (2011), "An analysis of the drivers affecting the implementation of green supply chain management", Resources, Conservation and Recycling, Vol. 55 No. 6, pp. 659-667

34. Eltayeb, T.K. and Zailani, S.H.M. (2009), "Going green through green supply chain initiatives towards environmental sustainability", Operations and Supply Chain Management, Vol. 2 No. 2, pp. 93

35. Emamisaleh, K., Rahmani, K., & Iranzadeh, S. (2018). Sustainable supply chain management practices and sustainability performance in the food industry. The South East Asian Journal of Management.

36. Epstein, M. J., & Roy, M. J. (2001). Sustainability in action: Identifying and measuring the key performance drivers. Long Range Planning, 34(5), 585-604.

37. er, R., Kim, D., & Bello, D. C. (2017). Relationship-based product innovations: Evidence from the global supply chain. Journal of Business Research, 80, 127-140.

38. Ferrer, G., & Whybark, D. C. (2000). From garbage to goods: Successful remanufacturing systems and skills. Business Horizons, 43(6), 55-64. Retrieved from https://www.proquest.com/scholarly-journals/garbage-goods-successful-remanufacturing-systems/docview/195368243/se-2

39. Fleischmann, M., Beullens, P., Bloemhof-Ruwaard, J.M. and Van Wassenhove, L.N. (2001). The impact of product recovery on logistics network design. Production & Opera-tions Management, 10, 156–173.

40. Fleischmann, M., Bloemhof-Ruwaard, J. M., Dekker, R., Van der Laan, E., Van Nunen, J. A., & Van Wassenhove, L. N. (1997). Quantitative models for reverse logistics: A review. European journal of operational research, 103(1), 1-17.

41. Furlan Matos Alves, Marcelo Wilson, Lopes de Sousa Jabbour, Ana Beatriz, Kannan, D., & Chiappetta Jabbour, C. J. (2017). Contingency theory, climate change, and low-carbon operations management. Supply Chain Management, 22(3), 223-236. doi:https://doi.org/10.1108/SCM-09-2016-0311

42. Gandhi, S., Mangla, S. K., Kumar, P., & Kumar, D. (2015). Evaluating factors in implementation of successful green supply chain management using DEMATEL: A case study. International strategic management review, 3(1-2), 96-109.

43. Gatersleben, B., Steg, L., & Vlek, C. (2002). Measurement and determinants of environmentally significant consumer behavior. Environment and Behavior, 34(3), 335-362.

44. Gifford, R., & Nilsson, A. (2014). Personal and social factors that influence pro- environmental concern and behaviour: A review. International Journal of Psychology, 49(3), 141-157. doi: 10.1002/ijop.12034

45. Gisela, A. D., Tomás Eloy, S. F., & Gloria, C. R. (2019). The relevance of green practices worldwide: An overview.

46. Goglio, P., Zamagni, A., & Farina, L. (2021). Assessing the environmental impact of products using life cycle assessment. Journal of Cleaner Production, 314, 128081. doi: 10.1016/j.jclepro.2021.128081

47. hang, J., & Liu, Y. (2021). Green technology innovation and sustainable development. Journal of Cleaner Production, 280, 124190. doi: 10.1016/j.jclepro.2020.124190

48. Hanna, M.D., Newman, W.R. and Johnson, P. (2000), "Linking operational and environmental improvement through employee involvement", International Journal of Operations & Production Management, Vol. 20 No. 2, pp. 148-65.

49. Hartmann, J., & Moeller, S. (2014). Chain liability in multitier supply chains? Responsibility attributions for unsustainable supplier behavior. Journal of operations management, 32(5), 281-294.

50. Hazaea, S. A., Ebrahim Mohammed Al-Matari, Zedan, K., Khatib, S. F. A., Zhu, J., & Amosh, H. A. (2022). Green purchasing: Past, present and future. Sustainability, 14(9), 5008. doi:https://doi.org/10.3390/su14095008

51. Hobson, K. A., Burke, I. C., & Pearse, P. H. (2006). Positive illusions and the management of the environment. Conservation Biology, 20(3), 617-619.

52. Hsu, C.W. and Hu, A.H. (2008), "Green supply chain management in the electronic industry", International Journal Environment Science Technology, Vol. 5 No. 2, pp. 205-216.

53. Hultman, M., & Luchs, M. (2021). Marketing sustainable technology: The role of distribution channels in creating consumer demand. Journal of Marketing, 85(3), 46-65. doi: 10.1177/0022242921996164

54. Jansson, J., Marell, A., & Nordlund, A. (2011). Psychological antecedents of environmental concern and behavior: A meta-analysis. Journal of Environmental Psychology, 31(3), 246- 254.

55. Jayaraman, V., Srivastava, R., & Benton, W. C. (1999). Supplier selection and order quantity allocation: a comprehensive model. Journal of Supply Chain Management, 35(1), 50-58.

56. Jha, A., Sharma, R., Kumar, V., & Verma, P. (2022). Designing supply chain performance system: A strategic study on indian manufacturing sector. Supply Chain Management, 27(1), 66-88. doi:https://doi.org/10.1108/SCM-05-2020-0198

57. Joshi, Y., & Rahman, Z. (2016). Predictors of young consumer's green purchase behaviour. Management of Environmental Quality, 27(4), 452-472. Retrieved from https://www.proquest.com/scholarly-journals/predictors-young-consumers-green-purchase/docview/1791019013/se-2

58. Kim, D., Parajuli, R., & Thoma, G. J. (2020). Life cycle assessment of dietary patterns in the united states: A full food supply chain perspective. Sustainability, 12(4), 1586. doi:https://doi.org/10.3390/su12041586

59. King, A.A. and Lenox, M.J. (2001), "Lean and green? An empirical examination of the relationship between lean production and environmental performance", Production and Operations Management, Vol. 10 No. 3, pp. 244-56.

60. Kleindorfer, P. R., Singhal, K., & Van Wassenhove, L.,N. (2005). 2020 Production and Operations Management, 14(4), 482-492. Retrieved from https://www.proquest.com/scholarly-journals/sustainable-operations- management/docview/228764679/se-2

61. Kleyner, A., & Stavins, S. (2018). Sustainable logistics: A strategic perspective. Journal of Cleaner Production, 189, 141-152.

62. Kogg, B., 2003. Power and incentives in environmental supply chain management. In: Seuring, S.A., Muller, M., Goldbach, M., Schneidewind, U. (Eds.), Strategy and Organization in Supply Chains. Springer.

63. Krikke, Hans Ronald (1998), Recovery Strategies and Reverse Logistic Network Design, Enschede, The Netherlands: University of Twente.

64. Kroon, L., & Vrijens, G. (1995). Returnable containers: an example of reverse logistics. International journal of physical distribution & logistics management, 25(2), 56-68.

65. Kumar, P., Scheibe, K. P., & Weber, C. (2020). Green packaging: A review of current practice and future directions. Journal of Cleaner Production, 254, 120085.

66. Liu, B. (2023). Integration of novel uncertainty model construction of green supply chain management for small and medium-sized enterprises using artificial intelligence. Optik, 273, 170411.

67. Lo, S. M., & Shiah, Y. A. (2016). Associating the motivation with the practices of firms going green: the moderator role of environmental uncertainty. Supply Chain Management: An International Journal.

68. Louwers, D., Kip, B. J., Peters, E., Souren, F., & Flapper, S. D. P. (1999). A facility location allocation model for reusing carpet materials. Computers & industrial engineering, 36(4), 855- 869.

69. Maruglio, B.W. (1991). Environmental Manage- ment Systems. New York: ASQC Quality Press.

70. Mirchandani, M. G., Johnson, G. M., & Bove, L. J. (1989). Task Order 2 Enhanced Preliminary Assessment, Fort Douglas, Salt Lake City, Utah. WESTON (ROY F) INC WEST CHESTER PA

71. Mohan, M., Singh, A., & Verma, V. (2017). A review of green purchasing literature: Trends and challenges. Journal of Cleaner Production, 161, 1-15.

72. Mollenkopf, D., & Dapiran, G. P. (2005). World-class logistics: Australia and new zealand. International Journal of Physical Distribution & Logistics Management, 35(1), 63- 74. doi:https://doi.org/10.1108/09600030510577430

73. Mostafa, M. M. (2007). Gender differences in Egyptian consumers' green purchase behaviour: the effects of environmental knowledge, concern and attitude. International journal of consumer studies, 31(3), 220-229.

74. Mostard, J., & Teunter, R. (2006). The newsboy problem with resalable returns: A single period model and case study. European Journal of Operational Research, 169(1), 81-96.

75. Pagell, M., & Shevchenko, A. (2014). Why research in sustainable supply chain management should have no future. Journal of Supply Chain Management, 50(1), 44-55

76. Pagiaslis, A., & Krontalis, A. K. (2014). Green purchasing practices of firms: A survey of the Greek market. Journal of Cleaner Production, 66, 441-450.

77. Peattie, K. (1999). Rethinking marketing: Shifting to a greener paradigm. In M. Charter & M. J. Polonsky (Eds.), Greener marketing: A global perspective on greening marketing practice (pp. 57-70). Sheffield, UK: Greenleaf.

78. Petljak, K., Zulauf, K., Štulec, I., Seuring, S., & Wagner, R. (2018). Green supply chain management in food retailing: Survey-based evidence in croatia. Supply Chain Management, 23(1), 1-15. doi:https://doi.org/10.1108/SCM-04-2017-0133

79. Pishvaee, M. S., Jolai, F., & Razmi, J. (2012). A stochastic optimization model for integrated forward/reverse logistics network design. Journal of Cleaner Production, 20(1), 61-71. Sarkis, J., Zhu, Q., & Lai, K. H. (2011). An organizational theoretic review of green supply chain management literature. International Journal of Production Economics, 130(1), 1-15.

80. Polonsky, M., Bhaskaran, S., & Cary, J. (2005). Exploring the opportunities for sustainable food labelling: a supply chain perspective.

81. Pujari, D., & Wright, G. (1996). Developing environmentally conscious product strategies: a qualitative study of selected companies in Germany and Britain. Marketing Intelligence & Planning, 14(1), 19-28.

82. Pullman, M., Maloni, M., & Carter, C. 2009, Food for thought: Social versus environmental sustainability practices and performance outcomes, Journal of Supply Chain Management, 45(4), 38 – 54.

83. Ravi, V., & Shankar, R. (2005). Analysis of interactions among the barriers of reverse logistics. Technological Forecasting and Social Change, 72(8), 1011-1029.

84. Russo, M. V., & Fouts, P. A. (1997). A resource-based perspective on corporate environmental performance and profitability. Academy of Management Journal, 40(3), 534- 559.

85. S. Lee, J. Sung, D. Choi and Y. Noh, "Pressures affecting green supply chain performance" Management Decision., vol. 51, no. 8, pp. 1753-1768, 2013.

86. Sahu, S., & Rao, K. N. (2021). The thematic landscape of literature on supply chain management in india: A systematic literature review. [Literature on supply chain management in India] Benchmarking, 28(3), 881-925. doi:https://doi.org/10.1108/BIJ-06-2020-0312

87. Sarkis, J., Zhu, Q. and Kee-hung, L. (2011), "An organizational theoretic review of green supply chain management literature", International Journal of Production Economics, Vol. 130 No. 1, pp. 1-15.

88. Sayed, M., Hendry, L. C., & Zorzini Bell, M. (2017). Institutional complexity and sustainable supply chain management practices. Supply Chain Management: An International Journal, 22(6), 542-563.

89. Setyaning, L. B., Wiguna, I. P. A., & Rachmawati, F. (2020, September). Developing activities of green design, green purchasing, and green transportation as the part of green supply chain management in construction sector. In IOP Conference Series: Materials Science and Engineering (Vol. 930, No. 1, p. 012001). IOP Publishing.

90. Shan, H., Li, Y., & Shi, J. (2020). Influence of supply chain collaborative innovation on sustainable d e v e l o p m e n t of supply chain: A study on C hinese enterprises. Sustainability, 12(7), 2978. doi:https://doi.org/10.3390/su12072978

91. Sharma, S., Baughn, C. C., & Mehta, R. (2021). The motivation for "green" consumption: The moderating role of environmental concern and awareness. Journal of Business Research, 122, 532-543. doi: 10.1016/j.jbusres.2020.08.005

92. Shen, B., Ding, X., Chen, L., & Chan, H. L. (2017). Low carbon supply chain with energy consumption constraints: Case studies from China's textile industry and simple analytical model. Supply Chain Management, 22(3), 258-269. Retrieved from https://www.proquest.com/scholarly-journals/low-carbon-supply-chain-with-energy-consumption/docview/1926834714/se-2

93. Spengler, T., Püchert, H., Penkuhn, T., & Rentz, O. (1997). Environmental integrated production and recycling management. European Journal of Operational Research, 97(2), 308- 326.

94. Srivastava, S.K., 2007. Green supply chain management: a state-of-the-art literature review. International Journal of Management Reviews 9, 53e80.

95. Stallkamp, C., Steins, J., Ruck, M., Volk, R., & Schultmann, F. (2022). Designing a recycling network for the circular economy of plastics with different multi-criteria optimization approaches. Sustainability, 14(17), 10913. doi:https://doi.org/10.3390/su141710913

96. Steg, L., de Groot, J. I. M., & Lurvink, J. (2014). Environmental values in post-materialist and materialist societies. Environmental Politics, 23(5), 717-736.

97. Stern, P. C., Dietz, T., Abel, T., Guagnano, G. A., & Kalof, L. (1999). A value-belief-norm theory of support for social movements: The case of environmentalism. Human Ecology Review, 6(2), 81-97.

98. Tan, K. C. (2002). Supply chain management: practices, concerns, and performance issues. Journal of Supply Chain Management, 38(4), 42-53.

99. Thøgersen, J. (2006). Norms for environmentally responsible behavior: An extended taxonomy. Journal of Environmental Psychology, 26(4), 247-261.

100. Vermeir, I., & Verbeke, W. (2006). Sustainable food consumption: Exploring the consumer "attitude-behavioral intention" gap. Journal of Agricultural and Environmental Ethics, 19(2), 169-194.

101. Xu, J., Yu, Y., Wu, Y., Zhang, J. Z., Liu, Y., Cao, Y., & Eachempati, P. (2022). Green supply chain management for operational performance: anteceding impact of corporate social responsibility and moderating effects of relational capital. Journal of Enterprise Information Management.

102. Yalabik, B., Petruzzi, N.C. and Chhajed, D. (2005), "An integrated product returns model with logistics and marketing coordination", European Journal of Operational Research, Vol. 161 No. 1, pp. 162-82.

103. Yoo, K. H., & Gretzel, U. (2021). From green to sustainable: The role of performance in green technology adoption. Journal of Business Research, 126, 731-739. doi: 10.1016/j.jbusres.2021.02.044

104. Yu, W., Chavez, R., Feng, M., & Wiengarten, F. (2014). Integrated green supply chain management and operational performance. Supply Chain Management: An International Journal, 19(5/6), 683-696.

105. Yu, W.; Ramanathan, R. An empirical examination of stakeholder pressures, green operations practices, and environmental performance. Int. J. Prod. Res. 2015, 53, 6390–6407.

106. Zhu, Q., Geng, Y., Fujita, T. and Hashimoto, S. (2010), "Green supply chain management in leading manufacturers: case studies in Japanese large companies", Management Research Review, Vol. 33 No. 4, pp. 380-392.

107. Zhu, Q.; Sarkis, J.; Lai, K. Confirmation of a measurement model for green supply chain management practices implementation. Int. J. Prod. Econ. 2008, 111, 261–273.

108. Zhu, Q.; Sarkis, J.; Lai, K. Institutional-based antecedents and performance outcomes of internal and external green supply chain management practices. J. Purch. Supply Manag. 2013, 19, 106– 117

Appendix

Questionnaire

Dear Sir/Madam

The questionnaire is prepared for the research study leading to Ph.D. in Management registered with GLS University, Ahmedabad. It is a sincere request to you to give unbiased and realistic answers to all these questions based on your expertise and experience to make the implication of this research high-yielding. The information/opinion/data given by you will be used exclusively for academic purposes. Looking forward to a positive response and kind support from your side.

Tripti Sharma

Section (A) - GSCM Awareness

Q.1. Are you aware of the concept of "Green Supply Chain Management"?

Mark only one oval

(Yes) (No)

Q.2. Is there any implementation of Green Supply Chain Management Practices in your Organization?

Mark only one oval

(Yes) (No)

Q.3. Stage of Implementation of Green Supply Chain Management in my organization

Mark only one oval

( ) Emergence Stage

( ) Initial stage (Authorized Sustainability Statement, adopted practice from 1 year - 2 year)

( ) Middle Stage (Authorized Sustainability Statement, Adopted practice from 2 year - 5 year)

( ) Advanced Stage (Fully applied and reported Authorized Sustainability Statement, Adopted practice from more than 5 years)

Q.4. Please indicate the level of agreement (on a given five-point scale) of your organization on the following factors for awareness that motivate to implement various green supply chain practices at the organizational level.

(1 = Strongly Disagree to 5 = Strongly Agree, please put √ sign wherever applicable.)

Sr. No	Statement	5	4	3	2	1
1.	The estimated advantage and consciousness of green supply chain management practices encourage my organization to apply of GSCM					
2.	Rising in new business opportunities after the application of green supply chain management encourages my organization to follow green practices					
3.	Awareness about GSCM plays a vital role in enhancing both existing and new employees in my organization					
4.	Advancement in technology makes my organization adopt green practices					
5.	Initiatives are made towards rectification of issues related to the implementation of Green practices					
6.	Social awareness or publicizing the initiative of a company doing a favor to society motivates my organization toward GSCM adoption					
7.	Environment protection is important company's survival in current times					

Section (B) – GSCM Factors/Drivers

Q.5. Please indicate the level of agreement (on a given five-point scale) of your organization on the following factors/drivers that motivate you to implement various green supply chain Practices at the organizational level.

(1 = Strongly Disagree to 5 = Strongly Agree, Please put √ a **sign wherever applicable.)**

Sr. No	Statement	5	4	3	2	1
A.	**Institutional Pressure**					
1.	The regular government examination is carried out which leads our organization to compliance with environmental regulations and laws					
2.	Constant audits are done by organizations for compliance with environmental regulations and laws					
3.	Taxes for environmental protection leads to the implementation of green practices					
4.	Enforcement of law for environmental protection leads towards implementation of green practices					
5.	Successful application o f GSCM practices by our competitors compel our organization to adopt Green Practices					
6.	Fines for environmental protection lead towards implementation of green practices					

Sr. No	Statement	5	4	3	2	1
B.	**Normative Pressure**					
7.	The upward set-up of supply chain supplier to manufacture encouraged my organization to adopt the green initiative					
8.	Applying best environmental practices leads to increasing market share					
9.	Customers' preference for green products encourages my organization to take green initiatives					
10.	Customers are considered strategic partners for collaboration on green issues					
11.	Export Market has an eminent role in the adoption of Green Practices					
12.	Market demand plays an enormous role in the adoption of Green Practices					
13.	Awareness about the eco- design of the product motives my organization towards adoption of GSCM					
14.	The demand customers for eco-design products encourages them to adopt Green practices					
15.	Cooperation of customers for a clean environment leads to adopting GSCM					
16.	Consumers' Preference for Environmental Consideration makes organizations adopt GSCM					
17.	Collaboration with suppliers for environmental sustainability leads promotes GSCM					
18.	Sharing responsibilities with suppliers encourages them to adopt more environmentally friendly behaviors					
19.	Green logistics in the current scenario is gaining importance					
C.	**Environmental Orientation**					
20.	The fundamental corporate value of the organization is the safeguard of environment encourage GSCM adoption					
21.	The continuous support of senior managers and top-level management motivates for implementation of GSCM					
22.	Top- level management dedication towards the application of green supply chain management within an organization leads to apply GSCM					
23.	The organizational process which is designed to minimize the use of Restriction of Hazardous Substance assures reduction of adverse environmental effects is achieved encourages the adoption of GSCM					
24.	Corporate Social responsibility encourages adopting GSCM					
25.	The priority of selecting those practices which involve environmental criteria encourages GSCM adoption					

Sr. No	Statement	5	4	3	2	1
26.	Adopting Green manufacturing activity increases the efficiency of my organization and motivates organization to follow GSCM practices					
27.	The policy of designing products in recyclable form has involved my company in going for GSCM					
28.	Organization's one- part accountability for processes related to environmental standards leads to following best green practices					

Section (C) – GSCM Practices

Q.6. Please indicate your organization's phase of implementation/consideration of the following green supply chain activities (GSCM) on the given five-point scale as given below:

(1 = Strongly Disagree to 5 = Strongly Agree, please put √ sign wherever applicable.)

Sr. No	Statement	5	4	3	2	1
A.	**Green Design**					
1.	My Organization has framed a proper structure of t h e standardized design of Our products for reducing energy consumption					
2.	My Organization has framed a proper structure of t h e standardized design of Our products for reducing the difficulty in processing					
3.	My organization follows a recyclable design that attains maximum reuse of Component					
B.	**Green Purchase**					
1.	Issues related to the procurement of material ensures the positive impact of a Human health organization					
2.	Raw material purchased show not be detrimental to t h e environment is the major factor considered by my organization					
3.	My organization has adopted a formal approach towards green purchasing or Green procurement.					
4.	My organization is always adapting just- in - time logistic systems for Supplier cooperation					
5.	My organization follow proper Quality check to produce the raw material					
6.	The initiative is taken by my organization to organize workshops/ seminars to Educate our suppliers GSCM					
7.	The selection of suppliers is done based on their performance through formal evaluation, using established guidelines and procedures for GSCM.					
8.	My organization provides specifications to the suppliers that include environmental requirements for purchased items.					

Sr. No	Statement	5	4	3	2	1
C.	**Green Manufacturing**					
1.	An appropriate budget allocation for the application of GSCM practices is done By the organization					
2.	In process design implementation environmental & efficiency criteria are integrated by my organization					
3.	Minimizes hazardous/toxic waste during manufacturing is always the priority of my organization					
4.	Environmental factors are taken into consideration while a selection of manufacturing process by my organization					
5.	During the manufacturing process optimization of the consumption of energy and material is considered by my organization					
D.	**Organizational Involvement**					
1.	Cross-functional cooperation of employees of several departments of my organization encourages to implement of GSCM					
2.	At our organization efforts are made to establish linkage between environmental objectives with our companies' corporate goals.					
3.	There is encouragement for departmental interaction and exchange of information with regard to activities like performance, environment, efficiency, and many More					
4.	My organization's Top Management is always committed tothe implementation of GSCM					
E.	**Green Marketing**					
1.	The eco-labeling /eco-logo is put into operation by my organization					
2.	Eco-friendly packaging and eco-friendly aspect relating to the advertisement of the product are mainly considered on a priority base by my organization.					
3.	Green marketing encourages increasing profit of the business					
4.	Eco-brand plays a vital role in following GSCM					
F.	**Green Distribution**					
1.	My organization in vehicle use Eco-Friendly refrigerants					
2.	In my organization operation of transport vehicles is done by giving importance to fuel efficiency					
3.	My organization and its supplier have strong cooperation on the common use Of transportation and warehouses					
G.	**Reverse Logistics**					
1.	My organization makes sure that it's purchased products that must contain green attributes such as recycled or reusable items.					

Sr. No	Statement	5	4	3	2	1
2.	A recycling program for manufacturing operations is included in my organization					
3.	A reverse logistics program is applied in stock planning by my organization					
4.	Recycling is considered an essential part by the manufacturers of sustainability Management					
5.	The policy of taking back packaging has involved companies going for GSCM					
6.	The trend of consideration of the end life of a company's product has increased due to GSCM					
7.	My organization recovers products and/or components from customers for repair and remanufacture.					
H.	**Customer Co-Operation**					
1.	My organization considers customers' preference for products advanced in environmental record.					
2.	My organization gives priority to t h e production of green products Considering customers want					
3.	Regular review of customers is collected to enhance product according to the need of the customer					
4.	The establishment of social conduct is done for the health and safety of customers					
5.	My organization gets a good amount of cooperation from the customer for implementing Eco-the design of a product					
6.	My organization gets a good amount of cooperation from t h e customer for Cleaner production					
7.	My organization gets a good amount of cooperation from customers for green purchasing					
I.	**Green Technology**					
1.	Green technology is cost-effective so more emphasis is given by my organization for adoption					
2.	Technology advancement for manufacturing process is always regarded vital by my organization.					
3.	My organization consider important to adopt Green technology as it paly vital role in reducing energy consumption					
4.	My organization consider important the adoption of green technology as it have less impact on the environment					
5.	My organization adopt green technology as it helps in practicing innovative power production techniques.					

Section (D) - GSCM Performances

Q.7. Please indicate your level of agreement/opinion (as per the given five points scale) for each of the following parameters of performance results from Green Supply Chain Management practices implementation in your organization.

(1 = Strongly Disagree to 5 = Strongly Agree, please put √ sign wherever applicable.)

Sr. No	Statement	5	4	3	2	1
A.	**Environmental Performance**					
1.	GSCM application results in to decrease in solid waste					
2.	GSCM application results in to decrease in air emission					
3.	GSCM application results in to decrease in water wastage					
4.	GSCM application results in to decrease in releasing harmful pollutants					
5.	GSCM application results in to increase in the Organization's Environmental condition					
6.	GSCM application results in to decrease in t h e utilization of harmful material					
7.	GSCM application reduces carbon footprints					
B.	**Financial Performance**					
8.	GSCM application results in to decrease in penalties for Environmental accidents					
9.	GSCM application has increased the sales growth of our company					
10.	GSCM application has reduced the cost of material purchasing					
11.	GSCM application has reduced fees for waste discharge					
12.	GSCM application has reduced fees for waste treatment					
13.	GSCM application results in an increase in profitability					
14.	GSCM application results in to decrease the occurrence of accidents					
C.	**Operational Performance**					
15.	GSCM application increases the quantity of goods delivered onTime					
16.	GSCM application results in a reduction of cost of energy usage					
17.	GSCM application results in a reduction of the scarp					
18.	GSCM application results in enhancing the quality					
19.	GSCM application in the reduction of inventory level					
D.	**Social Performance**					
20.	GSCM application increases corporate image					
21.	GSCM application helps organizations for fulfillment of cooperate social responsibility					

Sr. No	Statement	5	4	3	2	1
22.	GSCM application increases social image					
23.	GSCM application helps in reducing no environmental accident					
24.	GSCM application leads in gaining customer loyalty toward the organization					
25.	GSCM application helps to improve the quality of life and health of workers					

Section(E)- Demographic Profile of Respondents

1. Name of the Respondent

   ____

2. Organization Name

   ____

3. Employee Designation:

   ____

4. Type of organization you are working with

   Mark only one Oval

   ◯ Private Enterprise

   ◯ Public Enterprise

5. Association with organization

   Mark one oval only

   ◯ Less than 3 years

   ◯ 3-6 years

   ◯ 7-9 years

   ◯ Above 9 years

6. Contact No.(Optional)

   ____

7. E-mail Id

____

8. Age

Mark only one oval

- ◯ 18-28
- ◯ 29-38
- ◯ 39-48
- ◯ 49-58
- ◯ Above 58

9. Education

Mark only one oval.

- ◯ Up to higher secondary
- ◯ Graduation
- ◯ Post-Graduation
- ◯ Doctorate and above

10. Occupation

Mark only one oval

- ◯ Salaried
- ◯ Self-Employed
- ◯ Businessman
- ◯ Other (Please Specify)
- ◯ Other:

Brief Biodata of Author

Dr Tripti Sharma is a PhD holder of GLS School of Doctoral Research and Innovations, Ahmedabad. She is a unique and charismatic personality, a blend of banker and academician. In her professional career, she served the banking industry for 2 years and handled various departments of the bank as an assistant manager. She handled various departments of operations like Clearing, Cash, and front of the bank. She gained incredible experience in the verification process of various transactions related to Clearing, Cash, and front. She possesses multitasking skills and an enthusiastic approach to life. After she resigned from the bank, she joined the academic world in 2019.

As far as her academic career is concerned, she has been associated with private institutes across Ahmedabad. She worked as a visiting faculty in the Center of Management Studies and Research, at Ganpat University and LJ University. In her academic journey, she has taught subjects like Business Statistics, and Economics (Concepts of Micro and Macro Economics, Theory of Demand and Supply, Concept of Market Structure and Concept of Cost and Revenue, theories of money). Basics of Econometrics, Problem-Solving Techniques, Foundation of Statistics, Business Ethics and Corporate Governance at Ganpat University & MBA – Agriculture students in Micro Finance.

Presently, she working with Ahmedabad Institute of Technology as a GTU endorsed faculty. She helped in mentoring and shaping young minds in academic field. Technology. Subjects Management Accounting, Insurance Risk Management, Security Analysis and Portfolio Management, Financial Derivatives, Banking, Performance and Operations Management, Research Methodology and Intellectual Property Rights. She helped in mentoring and shaping young minds in academic field.

She is an energetic and efficient writer too. She has published a booked named as **CHRYSALIS** at global platform which added eminently the feather to her career.

Co-Author Bio

Dr. Avni Patel is a Management graduate with specialization in Finance. She holds a doctoral degree in Management and is currently guiding Doctoral Candidates at the GLS University. She has over 14 years of experience in Academics and 4 years in corporate. Her area of interests are Operations Management, Financial Services and Economics for Managers. She has published and presented several papers in national and international journals and conferences.

www.ingramcontent.com/pod-product-compliance
Lightning Source LLC
LaVergne TN
LVHW070934160826
845679LV00021B/1801

9798893229134